THE RESEARCH PROJECT BOOK

Over 100
research reporting models!

by
Nancy Polette

Pieces of Learning

CLC0218
ISBN 1-880505-34-7
Printed in the United States of America
1998 Published by Pieces of Learning
Second Edition Copyright © 1992 by Nancy Polette
Biography section by Virginia Mealy and Nancy Polette
Illustrated by Paul Dillon

Acknowledgements

Lines from THE ROSE IN MY GARDEN by Arnold Lobel © 1984 Greenwillow Books.

Jacket illustration from SHOES by Elizabeth Winthrop, illustrated by William Joyce © 1986 Harper Collins Publishers.

Jacket illustration and lines from HOW TO TURN WAR INTO PEACE by Louise Armstrong. Illus. by Bill Basso. © 1979 Harcourt, Brace, Jovanovich.

Lines from COME ALONG by Rebecca Caudill © 1969 Holt, Rinehart and Winston.

Lines from A HOUSE IS A HOUSE FOR ME by Maryann Hoberman, © 1978 Viking Press.

Jacket illustration for IF I WERE IN CHARGE OF THE WORLD by Judith Viorst, Illustrated by Lynne Cherry © 1982, Atheneum Publishers.

Jacket illustration for THE MICROSCOPE by Maxine Kumin. Illustrated by Arnold Lobel. © 1984, Harper Collins Publishers.

Jacket illustration for ANIMAL FACT, ANIMAL FABLE by Seymour Simon. Illustrated by Diane deGroat. © 1979 Crown Publishers.

Jacket illustration and lines from COMPUTER SENSE, COMPUTER NONSENSE by Seymour Simon. Illustrated by Steven Lindblom. © 1984, J . B. Lippincott Publishers

Jacket illustration for BODY SENSE, BODY NONSENSE by Seymour Simon. Illustrated by Dennis Kendrick. © 1981 J . B. Lippincott Publishers.

Illustration by Bob Marstall from THE LADY AND THE SPIDER by Faith McNulty. © 1986, Harper Collins Publishers.

Lines from THE BOOK OF PREDICTIONS by David Wallechinsky, Amy Wallace and Irving Wallace © 1980, William Morrow Publishers.

Jacket illustration for "THE EARTH IS FLAT"-AND OTHER GREAT MISTAKES by Laurence Pringle. Illustrated by Steve Miller. © 1984, William Morrow Publishers.

Jacket illustration and page 38 from Steven Caney's INVENTION BOOK included with permission of Workman Publishing, © 1985.

Illustration by Tom Huffman from VITAMINS-WHAT THEY ARE, WHAT THEY DO by Judith S. Seixas. © 1986, Greenwillow Books.

Illustrations by Robert Duffek for RE/USES by Carolyn Jabs. © 1982, Crown Publishers .

Illustration from DAKOTA DUGOUT by Ann Turner, Illustrated by Ronald Himler, © 1985, Macmillan Publishers.

Jacket illustration for GOING WEST by Martin Waddell. Pictures by Philippe Dupasquier © 1984, Harper Collins Publishers.

Jacket illustration for THE BELLS OF LONDON by Ashley Wolff. © 1985, Dodd Mead.

Illustration from THE OPTICAL ILLUSION BOOK by Seymour Simon, © 1984, Morrow Junior Books.

Jacket illustration for THE PRINCIPAL'S NEW CLOTHES by Stephanie Calmenson. Illustrated by Denise Brunkus.

Jacket illustration for MRS. TORTINO'S RETURN TO THE SUN by Shirley and Pat Murphy. © 1980, Lothrop, Lee & Shepard.

Jacket Illustration for TOWN AND COUNTRY by Alice and Martin Provensen. © 1987, Harper Collins Publishers.

Lines from A MOUSE'S DIARY by Michelle Cartlidge, © 1981 Lothrop, Lee & Shepard.

Lines from THE MAN WHOSE NAME WAS NOT THOMAS by M. Jean George, © 1981, Doubleday and Company.

Text and illustrations from THE LITTLE WORM BOOK by Janet and Allan Ahlberg, © 1979, Viking Press.

Illustration by Raymond Briggs for THE TIN POT FOREIGN GENERAL AND THE OLD IRON WOMAN, © 1985, Little-Brown Publishers.

Illustration from HOW LONG ? TO GO, TO GROW, TO KNOW by Ross and Patricia Olney. Illustrated by R .W . Alley. © 1984, William Morrow & Co.

Illustration from ENCYCLOPEDIA BROWN'S BOOK OF WACKY SPIES by Donald Sobol, illustrated by Ted Enik, © 1984 Morrow Junior Books.

THE RESEARCH PROJECT BOOK

TABLE OF CONTENTS

Introduction 1-6
Looking At Topic Ideas 7
PROJECTS TO BUILD A WORKING VOCABULARY 8
Reporting on Language with Photographs 9
Researching and Reporting On Items Within One Category 10
Researching Natural Settings Using the Cumulative Tale 11
Reporting on Careers and/or Occupations 12
Understanding Law Vocabulary 13
From Research To Riddles 14
POETRY PATTERNS 15
Reporting On A Non-Fiction Topic In Verse 16
A Poetry Journey 17
Poetry Patterns 18
Reporting History-The Narrative Poem 19
Reporting On Places 20
Reporting Research With Poetry 21
Reporting Discoveries in Verse 22
Combining Biography and Incidents from History 23
The Story Poem 24
Reporting A Wildlife Incident 25
MODELS FOR REPORTING FACTUAL INFORMATION 26
Research On One Topic 27
Fact Or Fable? 28
Reporting On One Aspect Of An Animal 29
A Sense And Nonsense Model 30
A True/False Model 31
A Five Senses Report 32
Reporting On An Encounter 33
Take A Trip Through... 34
A Guidebook To An Unusual Place 35
A Day In The Life Of... 36
A Letter-Writing Project 37
Causes and Effects 38
Predicting The Future 39
Great Mistakes 40
Biography Report 41
Turning Points! 42
Setting Criteria For A Collective Biography 43
Researching Personalities 44
You Can Build a Better Mousetrap! 45
Become An Inventor, Apply Flexible Thinking! 46
The How-They-Do-It Pattern 47
A How-To Model 48
How To Dig A Hole 49
Things To Do With Water 50
How A House Happens 51
Vitamins, What They Are, What They Do 52
Re-Uses 53
Products Requiring Flexible Thinking 54
The Newspaper Clipping Report 55-58
REPORTING WITH A CAMERA, PAINTS AND PENCIL 59
The Illustrated Or Photographic Essay 60
The Illustrated Dictionary 61
Observing An Animal 62

The Pictorial Journal 63
Researching Community Churches 64
Fooling Folks With Photographs 65
BLENDING FACT AND FICTION 66
Comparing Cultures With Folktales 67
Using Cartoons In Writing The How-To Book 68
Animal Habitats - The Riddle Poem 69
A Story Report 70
The Truth About... 71
Problem-Solving 72
If You Lived 73
Take An Unexpected Trip 74
Keep A Diary! 75
Contrasting Lifestyles 76
The Source Of Foods We Eat 77
Describing What A Thing Is Not! 78
Looking At History Through Other Eyes 79
The Five Chapter Book 80
History As Satire 81
RECORD BOOKS 82
A Book Of Averages 83
Decision-Making 84
Strange Facts 85
An Animal Record Book 86
Amazing Achievements 87
Record Books 88
Using Measurement As A Reporting Tool 89
A Book Of Wacky Facts 90
Animal Assistant 91
A Tic-Tac-Toe Report 92
The Letter Report 93
Project Planning: Hobbies 94
Biography Reports Without Copying 95-96
Happiness Is 97
Party Time 98
Write An Obit. 99
One Person, One Episode 100
Explanation Please (Inventors) 101
A Month In The Life Of. 102
Construct A Crossword 103
T-Shirt 104
Describing By Comparing 105
My Favorite Things 106
Time Capsule 107
Contemporaries 108
Life Problems 109
Extra! Extra! Read All About It 110
Super Sports (Heroes) 111
Leaders: Canadian and U. S. 112
Bio Poem 113
Musical Cinquains 114
Women And Duty. 115
Rebel Rousers 116
Mystery Person Biography Report #1 117
Mystery Person Biography Report #2 118
Television Show Biography Report 119-120
Selected Bibliography 121-124

The Research Project Book

by
Nancy Polette

Introduction

By about grade four, students in schools with library/media programs have, for the most part, achieved familiarity with the contents of their particular media center and have acquired most of the basic skills of location of library/media materials. It would follow then that by the end of grade four that independent study projects should be a basic part of the curriculum. However, regardless of the skills the student may possess, many research assignments do not call for the utilization of these skills. Teachers bemoan the fact that most students tend to copy information from the encyclopedia or the handiest reference book and that the majority of research assignments are not eagerly approached by students.

In traveling throughout the United States and Canada and in interviewing several hundred teachers a year it is this writer's guess that sixty to seventy percent of research projects carried out by students are at the *knowledge* or copying level. These same teachers who have been interviewed show both a willingness and a desire to move students from this initial copy stage to research projects which require analysis and synthesis of data as well as problem-solving and evaluation.

The key to moving students from lower to higher levels of thinking in the research activity is **product**. If we change the product we change the process the student uses to obtain the product. For example, if the student is asked to do a report on a particular state, the typical response is to copy several paragraphs about that state from the encyclopedia. The thinking level used is **knowledge**. When we change the product we also change the thinking level required. The assignment might be as follows: The White House has called and your family has been selected as the typical family for your state. The President is coming to dinner. Plan a menu. You may serve only those things raised or grown in your state. You may use only ingredients raised or grown in your state.

With the foregoing assignment the student must first locate the information. Second, he or she must analyze the information in order to combine separate elements in a new way (synthesis) to create a menu. Thus the higher levels of thinking are achieved through the changing of the research product.

Many teachers use picture books as patterns for creative writing. Non-fiction books can be used in the same way as patterns for those kinds of research projects which require not only the use of the skills of location and acquisition, but the development of divergent products based on the pattern in a particular book. Several examples follow.

BOOKS TO INTRODUCE THE VOCABULARY OF A TOPIC

Jane Howard's *When I'm Sleepy* (Dutton 1985) shows a little girl sleeping with a variety of animals. She is in a den with a bear, a nest with a bird and is shown in both the position and habitat of the animal. Young researchers might report on animal habits with books entitled *When I'm Hungry* or *When I Want to Play*. Their books would follow this pattern by showing or describing animals eating or at play.

The Rose in My Garden (Greenwillow 1984) by Arnold Lobel introduces flowering plants. Each page introduces a new plant and shows its location in relation to the rose. Students can use this model to write *The Shark in My Ocean* or *The Clam at My Seashore* or any other creature in its natural habitat. Special aspects of plant and/or animal life can be reported using the patterns found in *Slow Creatures* by Ernest Prescott (Watts 1976), *The Truth About the Moon* by Clayton Bess (Houghton Mifflin 1983), *What's That Noise?* by Michele Lemieux (Morrow 1985) or *A Bag Full of Pups* by Dick Gackenbach (Clarion 1981).

REPORTING ABOUT PEOPLE AND PLACES

Martin's Hats by Joan Blos (Morrow 1984) shows young Martin trying out a different hat on each page. Here is a great model for a guessing book. On one page the student could show the shoe, or workplace, or vehicle of a particular worker and let the reader guess the owner. The next page could show the owner and tell a little about that particular occupation.

In *Mrs. Huggins and Her Hen Hannah* (Dutton 1985) author Lydia Dabcovich shows many of the tasks that must be done on a farm. Using this same idea the student can create a character and the character's pet and show the tasks that would be performed in a lighthouse, or a weather station, a firehouse or on a ranch.

BIOGRAPHY/HISTORY

A variety of product models exist to add excitement to research in both history and biography. One of the best is the narrative poem. After researching the life of a famous person or the facts of an historical event, writing a narrative poem about the person or event can be an exciting challenge. Two excellent examples for students to see as models are *The Microscope* by Maxine Kumin (Harper & Row, 1984) which tells of the life of Anton Leeuwenhoek, and *Paul Revere's Ride* by Henry Wadsworth Longfellow (Illustrated by Nancy Winslow Parker, Greenwillow, 1985). Another excellent model for reporting history is Judith Viorst's *If I Were in Charge of the World* (Atheneum, 1983). In this poem the author muses about how things would be added, or cancelled if she were in charge of the world. The same pattern can be used for reporting places or events in history. *If I Were in Charge of a Wagon Train on the Oregon Trail* or *If I Were in Charge of the Mayflower* are examples of topics.

Many models of "How To" books abound. These can be analyzed to get ideas for the format of the student's own "how to" book: *How to Dig a Hole to the Other Side of the World* by Faith McNulty (Harper & Row 1979), *How a House Happens* by Jan Adkins (Walker 1972) *Steve Caney's Invention Book* (Workman 1985) *Lights, Camera, Action* by Gail Gibbons (Crowell 1985).

REPORTING IN PICTURES

For students who have problems with the written report, the photo essay can be an excellent means of reporting information. Photographs with a camera or illustrated picture essays can be done. Good examples of product models are: *Animals of Course: Mouths, Noses, Feet and Eyes* by Jill Bailey (Grossett 1985), *Going West* by Martin Waddell (Harper & Row 1984) and *Watching Foxes* by Jim Arnosky (Lothrop 1985).

RECORD BOOKS

Most students are familiar with the GUINNESS BOOK OF WORLD RECORDS and are eager to try compiling their own record books. A record book can be made on any topic from animals to space travel. Good examples of record books for students to study are *How High Is Up* by Bernice Kohn, a book of interesting questions and answers; *How Long ? To Go, To Grow, To Know* by Ross and Patricia Olney (Morrow 1984) and *In One Day* by Tom Parker which tells many things which happen in one day in the United States.

Using these patterns students could do a record book about their class. Each class member has been somewhere, done something, has a hobby, knows something, that no one else can claim. Ambitious classes might do an *In One Day* book about the school, keeping records of all kinds for two or three weeks on as many aspects of the school as possible. For example: How many pencils are sharpened in our school in one day? How many times does the phone ring? How many students are late?

A quick survey of library/media collections will reveal many more product models that will serve as patterns for changing students' research products. In combining the research process with the opportunity to produce something new students cannot help but gain both knowledge of the skills and information needed and of themselves as creative individuals. *The Research Project Book* will start students on the road to productive research and serve as a guide for these creative and productive projects.

The purchaser is allowed limited reproduction rights of thirty (30) copies of activity pages in this book for instructional use only.

LOOKING AT TOPIC IDEAS

Before you determine one specific topic for research it is often useful to examine several topics in terms of past, present and future.

Example: AN APPLE

     IT WAS <u>once a seed in the ground</u>
     IT IS <u>a delicious edible fruit</u>
     IT COULD BE <u>applesauce, apple pie</u>

Play with several topic ideas in this way by completing the boxes below. Select the one which most appeals to you. You now have a framework for your project - a beginning, a middle and an end.

TOPIC	IT WAS...	IT IS...	IT COULD BE...

PROJECTS TO

BUILD A

WORKING

VOCABULARY

REPORTING ON LANGUAGE WITH PHOTOGRAPHS

The creators of the book PUNIDDLES have combined two photographs to illustrate a simple word.

You can do the same either by taking your own photographs or by finding pictures in old magazines to cut out and combine in new ways.

PUNIDDLES

pun•id•dle (pŭn•ĭd'•l)

n. 1. A pair of photographs that suggest a literal or obvious solution in a punny way. 2. *pl.* A game using the pair of photographs to deduce the punny solution. [Source: pun, riddle]

Bruce and Brett McMillan
Photography by Bruce McMillan

Houghton Mifflin Company, Boston 1982

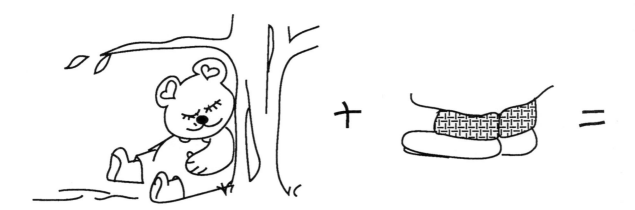

List as many compound words as you can. How many can you illustrate with pairs of photographs? Make your own book of puniddles!

_____ _____   _____ _____

_____ _____   _____ _____

_____ _____   _____ _____

_____ _____   _____ _____

_____ _____   _____ _____

_____ _____   _____ _____

_____ _____   _____ _____

A Bag Full of Pups

By Dick Gackenbach
Clarion Books 1981

RESEARCHING AND REPORTING ON ITEMS WITHIN ONE CATEGORY

In this book, Mr. Mullens has a bag full of pups to give away. Those who take the pups do so because each dog provides a specific service for its new owner. These owners are:

A Dairy Farmer

A Magician

A Blind Person

A Lonely Lady

A Fireman

A Policeman

A Grocer

A Dog Trainer

A Hunter

1. Name as many of one kind of animal as you can. (birds, fish, cats)

2. Group those you named by the way in which they are useful to man.

3. Think about a story in which you bring the bird, fish or animal together with a person who needs it.

Possible Titles

A Stable Full of Horses

An Ocean (or Lake or River) Full of Fish

A Backyard Full of Insects

A Zoo Full of Snakes

A Forest Full of Birds

RESEARCHING NATURAL SETTINGS
USING THE CUMULATIVE TALE

THE ROSE IN MY GARDEN is a wonderful introduction to the flowering world! Each new flower appears on a new page and is added to those which appeared earlier. At the end of the book we see the entire garden.

Select an environmental setting. This might be an ocean, a desert, a mountain, a seashore, a lake, a forest or woodland or any other setting you wish to research.

Research the setting you have chosen. Make lists of the many living and non living things found in that setting. Note the **order** found in the setting. Which things are usually found together?

Decide on the one living or non-living thing you will choose to begin your cumulative tale. What happens to that thing? How can adding other elements of the environment help the first thing you mention in some way? What surprise ending will you use for your story?

THE ROSE IN MY GARDEN
ARNOLD LOBEL
Pictures by ANITA LOBEL

"This is the rose in my garden. This is the bee that sleeps on the rose in my garden."

And so begins the horticultural panoply— a cumulative verse involving hollyhocks, marigolds, zinnias, daisies, bluebells, lilies, peonies, pansies, tulips, and sunflowers— and a surprise.

Possible Topics To Research

The Jellyfish in My Ocean

The Clam At My Seashore

The Rattlesnake in My Desert

The Fir Tree on My Mountain

The Seed in the Farmer's Field

The Catfish in My Lake

The Trout in My River

The Woodchuck in My Woodland

The Desk in My Classroom

The Worm in My Backyard

THE ROSE IN MY GARDEN is published by Greenwillow Books, 1984.

FINDING A FOCUS IN RESEARCHING AND REPORTING ON CAREERS AND/OR OCCUPATIONS

In this model the author describes many different kinds of shoes. Think of different workers and the shoes they wear. Why do you think different workers wear different kinds of shoes?

HOW TO WRITE YOUR BOOK

1. Select four to six workers who need special shoes for the jobs they do.

2. Find books about those workers and read them.

3, DRAW A CONCLUSION! Why do you think each worker you read about wears his or her particular shoe?

4. Draw a picture of each worker's shoes on separate pages.

5. For each shoe that you draw, write three sentences telling who wears the shoe and why.

6. Add more illustrations if you wish. Where does the worker work? Draw a picture of the worker.

7. Your book might be a guessing book. Draw a picture of the shoes and ask your reader who wears this particular shoe. On the next page show who wears the shoe and tell why.

8. You may want to do other books about occupations and the special tools, hats, vehicles or workplaces.

A Child's Guide To Conflict Resolution

HOW TO TURN WAR INTO Peace

by Louise Armstrong
illustrated by Bill Basso

Harcourt, Brace, Jovanovich 1979

UNDERSTANDING LAW VOCABULARY

By telling of a disagreement between two children building sandcastles on a beach, Louise Armstrong illustrates the vocabulary of conflict.

The story begins:
This is Susie. If she's building her sandcastle right next to yours, you're in a POTENTIAL TROUBLE SPOT. Susie's digging might clog your moat creating an INCIDENT. If you yell, "move!" — you have a DISPUTE.

Susie is your ADVERSARY.

Study the way in which this author cleverly introduces the vocabulary of conflict. Below are words dealing with rules and laws.

CREATE AN ILLUSTRATED STORY WHICH INTRODUCES THIS VOCABULARY OF LAW AND RULES

accused	fairness	minors
authority	freedom	petition
bail	impartiality	power
citizens	judge	press
correction of wrongs	juris prudence	privacy
court	jury	property
due process	justice	protection
equality	laws	regulations
equal protection	lawyer	responsibility
equity	legal system	rights
		rules

FROM RESEARCH TO RIDDLES!

USING RIDDLE MAKING TO BUILD WORD POWER!

The more you know about a topic, the more riddles you can make.

Here is the secret for writing riddles:

1. Choose a topic and make a long list of as many words as you can that are associated with that topic.

    Example: Topic: *pigs*   words: (*ham, pen, pork slop, Porky, swine swill, mud, porcine, sow, shoat, piglet*)

2. Choose one or two short words from your list and remove the beginning letter or beginning blend.
    Example: ham — remove the *h* and you have *am*
    slop— remove the *sl* and you have *op*

3. List as many words as you can which begin with the letters *am*. List words that begin with the letters *op*. Examine your lists.

4. Write your riddles: put back the missing letter(s) for the answer.
    Example: What takes a pig to the hospital? A *ham*bulance

    What do you call a pig that works for the phone company?   a *slop*erator.

Try writing riddles based on a topic you have researched.

POETRY
PATTERNS

REPORTING ON A NON-FICTION TOPIC
IN VERSE

Work with a partner to guess the answers to these questions. Then listen to the poem to support or deny your guesses.
    A.   How many different kinds of fish are there? 10,000   20,000   30,000
    B.   How long is the smallest adult fish? $1/2$ inch   1 inch 3 inches 4 inches
    C.   How long is the largest adult fish? 10 feet   24 feet   30 feet   40 feet
    D.   How many years can an eel live?10 years   20 years   40 years   50 years
    E.   The largest fish ever caught on a rod and reel weighed?
             30 lbs. 50 lbs. 300 lbs. 360 lbs.

Fishy fishy in the brook
Daddy caught him with a hook
Mama fried him in a pan
Baby ate him like a man.
                What kind of fish could it be?
                Of 30,000 in pond and sea,
                Was he a Goby (only $1/2$ inch),
                Or a 40 foot shark to make folks flinch?

                        Or the long-lived 50 year old eel,
                        Or the sturgeon caught with rod and reel
                        360 pounds in weight,
                        Is that the fish that baby ate!!!

What topic might you research to tell about in verse?
What important facts can you include?
How will you illustrate your book?
Study this model carefully for ideas!

A POETRY JOURNEY

COME ALONG
By Rebecca Caudill
Illustrated by Ellen Haskin
Holt, Rinehart and Winston, 1969

The author takes the reader through the seasons, the mountain, and the meadow. She uses Haiku verse to give the reader vivid descriptions.

> "Two doves in a wood
> Coo softly to each other
> Celebrating spring."

Haiku verse consists of seventeen syllables. Lines one and three each contain five syllables and line two contains seven syllables.

Take A Trip

Take your reader on a trip using the model of Haiku verse above.

Possible trips

up a mountain   out to sea
across the tundra   into the desert
into the ocean depths   up into the sky

What to do:
1. Decide what kind of trip you want your reader to take through your writing.

2. Read about the area you wish to use.

3. List several words describing the area.

4. Organize your words into Haiku verse using this model.

5. Write a story using Haiku verse and illustrate as many scenes as possible.

A House is a House for Me

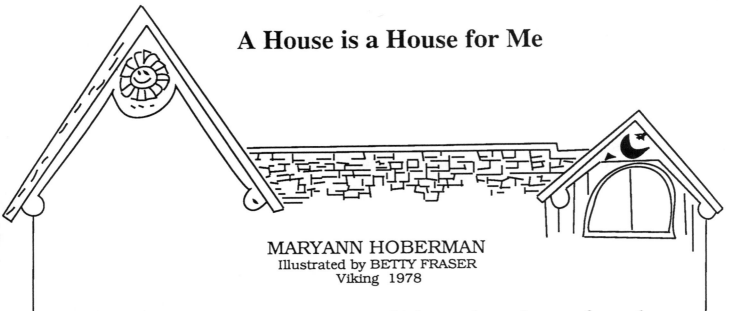

MARYANN HOBERMAN
Illustrated by BETTY FRASER
Viking 1978

POETRY PATTERNS

In her delightful book-length poem, Mary Ann Hoberman explores houses used by many of the Earth's creatures.

"A kennel is a house for a dog,
A dog is a house for a flea.
But when the dog strays,
The flea sometimes stays,
And then it may move in on me!"

Use this poetry model to research and report on what the Earth's creatures eat. Choose six to eight creatures for your poem.

EXAMPLE

_____ is a food for a cat.

_____ is food for a bee.

_____ is food for a worm.

but _____ is food for a me.

A _____ likes to eat _____ .

A _____ eats up some _____ .

A _____ prefers _____ and _____ .

But I like to eat _____ _____ .

Paul Revere's Ride

HENRY WADSWORTH
LONGFELLOW
Pictures by
NANCY WINSLOW PARKER
Greenwillow, 1985

Since it was written in 1863, generations of children have read, recited and loved Longfellow's classic poem. Here is the full text of this dramatization of an important incident in America's history, profusely and lovingly illustrated for young readers. With each turn of the page the excitement and adventure increase, and the heroic cadences of the poem are perfect for reading aloud again and again.

THE NARRATIVE POEM

AN EXCITING WAY TO REPORT ON EVENTS FROM HISTORY!
Paul Revere's Ride
by
Henry Wadsworth Longfellow

• • •

Listen, my children, and you shall hear
Of the midnight ride of Paul Revere,
On the eighteenth of April, in Seventy-five
Hardly a man is now alive
Who remembers that famous day and year.

He said to his friend, "If the British march
By land or sea from the town tonight,
Hang a lantern aloft in the belfry arch
Of the North Church tower as a signal light.

• • •

Longfellow (with the help in this book of Nancy Winslow Parker's illustrations) tells of this famous ride with all of its events in the form of a narrative poem.

Read the entire poem.

Note how each event is presented.

Research an important event from history.

List facts in the order in which they should appear.

Use *Paul Revere's Ride* as a model, write your narrative poem. (Often, schools discard older history textbooks. If these are available you can illustrate your poem with photographs or drawings from these texts.)

REPORTING ON PLACES

The place where one lives as either a child or an adult can be important to that person's life. The sights and sounds at Buckingham Palace would be very different from the sights and sounds at Thomas Jefferson's Monticello.

Research the home of a famous person or the location of an event from history. Write about it using the pattern below.

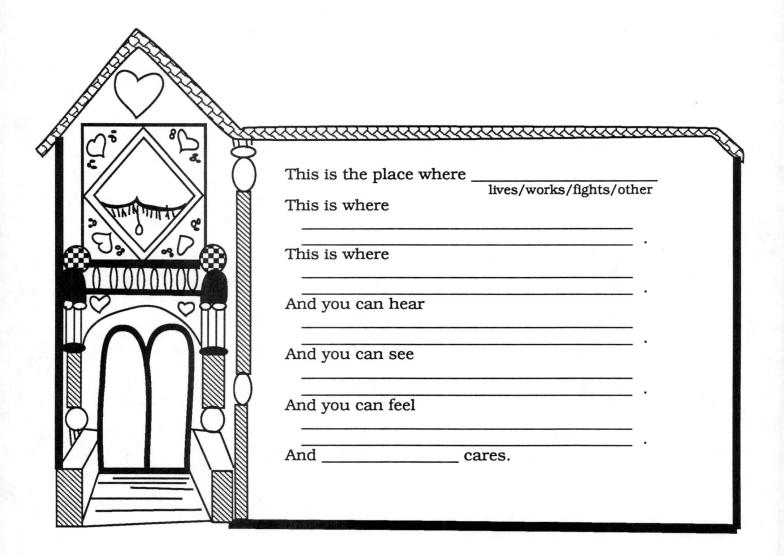

This is the place where _____
                                    lives/works/fights/other

This is where

_____

_____ .

This is where

_____

_____ .

And you can hear

_____

_____ .

And you can see

_____

_____ .

And you can feel

_____

_____ .

And _____ cares.

REPORTING RESEARCH WITH POETRY!

In the introductory poem in this fun collection Judith Viorst plays with the idea of what she would do if she were in charge of the world. In the poem the poet:

    Cancels four things
    Adds three things
    Tells five things "you
       wouldn't have"
    And ends with three
       things that might
       happen.

IF I WERE IN CHARGE OF THE WORLD

and other worries

poems for children and their parents by
JUDITH VIORST
ILLUSTRATED BY LYNNE CHERRY

Atheneum, ©1982

Using this poem as a reporting model, research one thing you would like to be in charge of: (The Mayflower? The space shuttle? Your state?)

If I were in charge of _____

I'd cancel	There'd be	You wouldn't have
_____	_____	_____
_____	_____	_____
_____	_____	_____
_____	_____	_____

Add a final verse telling what else *might* happen!

REPORTING DISCOVERIES IN VERSE!

With lighthearted humor, author and artist re-create for young readers Leeuwenhoek's bustling 17th century Dutch world as well as the small, fascinating, never-before-seen world his own microscopes revealed.

Anton Leeuwenhoek
was Dutch.
He sold pincushions,
cloth, and such.
The waiting townsfolk
fumed and fussed,
as Anton's dry goods
gathered dust.
He worked,
instead of tending store,
at grinding special lenses
for a microscope.

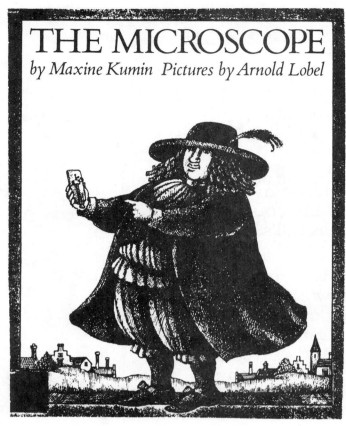

Harper & Row , Publishers
Jacket art © 1984 by Arnold Lobel

How many discoveries can you name in any category below?

agriculture
astronomy
anthropology
biology
exploration
medicine
psychology
technology
transportation
communication

Category: _____

Discoveries: _____

_____

_____

_____

_____

Select one discovery. Who made the discovery? Research that person's life and work. Recreate the discovery in verse form for others to enjoy.

COMBINING BIOGRAPHY AND INCIDENTS FROM HISTORY

Often, incidents in the lives of famous people give clues to their personalities and to their later accomplishments.

Below is an acrostic poem which describes an incident in the life of Winston Churchill. From reading about this incident, an assumption might be made that the abilities of being able to size up a situation and the courage to risk success played an important part in Churchill's later accomplishments as Prime Minister of Great Britain during World War II.

Use this model to report an incident in the life of another famous person.

W ar correspondent
I n South Africa, 1899
N ortorious Boer enemy
S eizes armored
T rain
O f those aboard, he is captured.
N o hope of escape.

C hecks out prison camp.
H igh walls, floodlights, sentries.
U p, over the wall, in an unguarded moment
R acing heart, he scales the heights.
C amp left behind.
H opping railroad cars
I n dead of night finds British help.
L auded as a hero.
L eader of the future.

THE STORY POEM

Here is an acrostic poem relating an incident in the childhood of George Gershwin. He grew up in a non-musical family on New York's east side. To survive there he had to be a fighter. He disliked school in general and music class in particular. Yet, George Gershwin, who became one of the world's most beloved composers, credited his entrance into the world of music with an incident that happened to him at the age of ten. The poem below relates this event.

Growing up, picking fights,
Ear for music, NONE!
Only sissies play pianos
Rubenstein was one.
Going past the arcade, Melody in F
Entered George's hearing, stopped by Treble Clef!

Going past school window, music from within
Enchanted by a melody, played on violin.
Rooted to the spot, hearing tiny Maxie play
Sad and haunting melody, George again was forced to stay.
He made friends with the fiddler, and at the age of ten
Worlds of music opened, he studied hard and then
Intensely innovative music flowed forth from his heart
NOW lauded by the critics, a composer set apart.

Read about Gershwin's life. The road to fame was not easy! Using the acrostic form above, relate another incident that may have been a turning point in his life.

REPORTING A WILDLIFE INCIDENT

Read;
DEER AT THE BROOK
by Jim Arnosky
Lothrop, 1986.

This is a beautiful book about watching the deer as it comes to the brook to drink. Arnosky is a careful observer of nature and includes many details that the less observant might miss.

1.   Be a patient observer. Observe the animal, worm, bird or insect you have chosen very carefully. Take notes on its behavior for one or more weeks.

2.   Look for behavior that is repeated. Ask yourself why it is repeated. What happens to the creature before or after the behavior?

3.   Write a story in words and pictures telling of a typical day in the creature's life.

4.   If possible, begin your story by telling of a problem the creature has. End the story by solving the problem.

MODELS

FOR

REPORTING

FACTUAL

INFORMATION

RESEARCH ON ONE TOPIC

Do you have a favorite animal or one you would like to know more about? What questions do you want to have answered? Write them on the lines below.
Where is the best place to find the answers?

      Encyclopedia?   A book about the bird or animal?

How will you illustrate your book?

      Drawings?   Photographs?   Pictures cut from old magazines?

How will you report the information?

      You might ask the question on one page and give the answer on the next.

List your favorite topic _____

What ten interesting questions will you answer for your reader?

  1. _____
  2. _____
  3. _____
  4. _____
  5. _____
  6. _____
  7. _____
  8. _____
  9. _____
10. _____

Use one page to answer each question in words and pictures. Design a title page and staple your book together for others to enjoy.

FACT OR FABLE?

Here is a colorful and informative picture book to test your knowledge about animals.

Each page poses a question which is answered on the next page.

In this book you will discover whether these and other statements are fact or fable.

Crown Publishers 1979

Bats are blind.
Some bees sting only once.
An owl is a wise bird.
The archer fish shoots down its food.
A turtle can walk out of its shell.
Some fish can climb trees.
A wolf lives alone.
Camels store water in their humps.

<u>What to do:</u>

1. Begin researching "truths" that parents often say.
   Example: *If you eat your bread crusts you can whistle.*
   Spinach will make you strong.

2. Collect as many sayings as you can from friends.

3. Discover whether the saying is fact or fable.

4. Using Seymour Simon's ANIMAL FACT/ANIMAL FABLE as your guide, write and illustrate your book. On one page give the saying. On the next page tell whether it is fact or fable and give an explanation.

5. Share your book with others.

REPORTING ON ONE ASPECT OF AN ANIMAL

SLOW CREATURES
By Ernest Prescott
Franklin Watts, 1976

All animals must eat to stay alive. They must also protect themselves from other animals. To do these things most creatures have something special about them. Elephants are big. Lions are strong. Antelopes are fast.

But what about creatures who are slow? Can being slow have its good points? A snail is slow, but it has a hard shell to protect itself. A chameleon is a slow moving lizard, but it can change colors to hide from its enemies. The Gila monster is slow but uses poison to attack his enemies. Some animals may be slow but have effective ways to protect themselves.

Can you think of a group of animals who have something in common? Create an informative booklet of these creatures.

Possible Topics

Fast Creatures
Creatures who live in the ocean
Creatures who live in the jungle
Creatures who live in the desert
Creatures who live in the lake
Creatures which change colors

What to do:

1. Choose ten animals from the same category.

2. Write the interesting facts about the animals.

3. Use illustrations or cut out pictures of these animals from magazines to use in your booklet.

A SENSE AND NONSENSE MODEL

Seymour Simon has used the subject of computers for an interesting and most informative true/false book.

The book contains twenty-four statements about computers and challenges the reader to decide whether each statement is sense or nonsense.

Some of the provocative statements are:
   Computers can take over the world.
   Computers never forget.
   Computer's can't see, hear or talk.
   Computers can smell flowers.

COMPUTER SENSE COMPUTER NONSENSE

Seymour Simon

Illustrated by Steven Lindblom

J.B. Lippincott 1984

1.   Select a subject of interest to you.

2.   Read about the subject.

3.   Make notes of unusual or interesting information.

4.   Decide how many sense and nonsense statements will be in your book. Be sure to include both.

5.   Use one page to write and illustrate a statement.

6.   Use the next page to explain whether the statement is sense or nonsense.

by
Seymour Simon

illustrated by
Dennis Kendrick

J.B. Lippincott   New York

A TRUE/FALSE
MODEL

Write your own true/false book using as your model Seymour Simon's, BODY SENSE, BODY NONSENSE.

In this book the author asks the reader whether a statement is sense or nonsense. On the next page the answer and an explanation are given.

Examples:

Sense or Nonsense?

An apple a day keeps the
    doctor away.
Redheads have bad tempers.
    Drafts cause colds.
Fish is brain food.

Pick a topic: Write your own Sense or Nonsense Book.

Science
Bird Sense, Bird Nonsense
Mammal Sense, Mammal
    Nonsense
Planet Sense, Planet Nonsense
Chemistry Sense, Chemistry
    Nonsense
Dinosaur Sense, Dinosaur
    Nonsense
Atomic Sense, Atomic
    Nonsense
Sound Sense, Sound Nonsense

History/Geography
Desert Sense, Desert Nonsense
U. S. Sense, U. S. Nonsense
Canadian Sense, Canadian
    Nonsense
Gold Rush Sense, Gold Rush
    Nonsense
WW II Sense, WW II Nonsense
People Sense, People Nonsense

A FIVE SENSES REPORT

In her book, SCIENCE EXPERIENCES: THE HUMAN SENSES, (Franklin Watts, 1968) Jeanne Bendick tells how we learn by using our five senses.

When we find ourselves in a new place, we learn about that place by SEEING SIGHTS, HEARING SOUNDS, SMELLING ODORS, TASTING FOOD and TOUCHING OBJECTS.

In your report you can help others to experience new places by describing sights, sounds, tastes, smells and feelings.

<u>A Circus</u>

Color:	A circus is many bright colors.
Looks like:	It looks like a patchwork quilt.
Sounds like:	It sounds like six record players going all at once.
Smells like:	It smells like sawdust.
Tastes like:	It tastes like cotton candy.
It makes me feel like:	It makes me feel like laughing.

<u>Choose</u>

A zoo

A firehouse

A hospital

A bakery

A post office

A grocery store

Read about the place you choose.

<u>Write your report.</u>

_____
Title

Color:_____

Looks like: _____

Sounds like: _____

Smells like: _____

Tastes like: _____

It makes me feel like: _____

_____

The Lady and the Spider
by Faith McNulty
illustrated by Bob Marstall

Harper & Row, Publishers
1986

REPORTING ON AN ENCOUNTER

A spider has made her home among the green hills and valleys of a lettuce leaf. It is a perfect den, just the right size, with a dewdrop pool nearby that will catch moths on moonlit nights. What the spider cannot know is that her home is in a lady's garden.

Each day the lady comes to pick lettuce for her lunch. Each day she comes a little closer to the spider's cozy nook without ever guessing that her giant footsteps shake the spider's little home.

Then one day the lady picks the very head of lettuce in which the spider lives. When at last she notices the spider frantically trying to escape, the lady stops just short of carelessly destroying the tiny creature and begins to marvel at its fragile existence — and to think about the miracle of things large and small.

What encounters have **you** had that you want to share with others? Have you met a person you would like to tell about? Did you observe something very interesting that you want to relate?

In describing **your** encounter consider:

1. When and where did the encounter take place?

2. How old were you at the time?

3. What did you see, hear, feel?

4. How did the encounter affect you?

5. What could others learn from reading about this encounter?

If you prefer to report your information in a different format, consider making a tape with background music to play for your class or audience. If you have slides of a trip you have taken you may want to write a script which blends fact and fiction to accompany the slides.

What's That Noise?
MICHELE LEMIEUX

Waking from a deep sleep, Brown Bear wonders, What's that noise? It's not the *squeak-squeak* that little mice make or the peep-peep of baby birds in their nests. It's not the noise the frogs by the stream make or the *chock-chock* of the woodsman's ax. What is that noise? Through the shady green of a springtime forest, the sunlit fields of summer, and the golden harvest of fall, the curious bear searches and finds a wonderful surprise. Young children everywhere will share the bear's delight in his own special moment of self-discovery.
Morrow Junior Books, 1985

TAKE A TRIP THROUGH ...

Use this model to take your readers on a trip through a particular environment and motivate readers to **want** to take the trip by allowing them to find something unusual at the end of the journey!

Possible Trips
Journey To The Moon
Journey To The Ocean Floor
Journey To Mr. MacGregor's
    Garden
Journey Through A Desert
Journey Through A Coal Mine
Journey Through A Pyramid
Journey To Epcot Or Disney World
Journey Through A Department
    Store
Journey Through A Police Station
Journey On The Oregon Trail
Journey Through Another State
Journey Through Another Country

What to do:

1. Read, read, read about your topic!

2. List all of the important words or ideas you want to present to your reader.

3. Place your words or ideas in the order in which you want to present them.

4. Decide on a main character for your story.

5. Decide what that character will be seeking.

6. Decide where the thing being sought will be found.

7. Write your story taking your character through each part of the trip.

8. Make the ending (when the object is found) a surprise.

9. Illustrate your story if possible.

A GUIDE BOOK TO AN UNUSUAL PLACE

In THE NOVA SPACE EXPLORER'S GUIDE, author Richard Maurer unfolds NOVA'S journey into space with more than 200 photographs and illustrations.

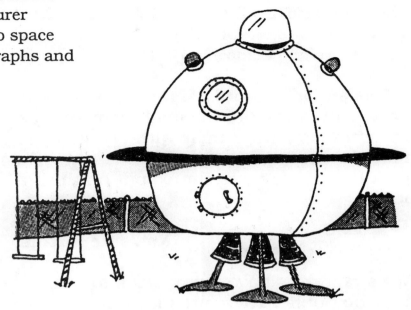

After an introduction to rockets past and present, the reader climbs aboard a space ship for a fabulous visit to lunar mountains, Mercury's volcanos, the outer planets of Jupiter and Pluto, and continues on into the galaxy to tour the stars.

Throughout this breath-taking trip, details of the space flight are given, including equipment needed and living arrangements.

Have you recently taken a trip?

Do you plan to take a trip soon?

Is your family involved in an unusual business that others might want to know about?

Write and illustrate a guidebook for **your** reader. Remember, details are very important to give your reader a clear view of the place you are describing.

Write And Illustrate A Guidebook

Consider:
The Zoo Explorer's Guide
The Fire House Explorer's Guide
The Library Explorer's Guide
An Explorer's Guide to Our Town
An Explorer's Guide to the Local Shopping Center

Choose one of the topics above or select your own topic.

Be sure to tell:
1. Where the reader is going, what special clothing or equipment he or she will need, and how long the trip will be.
2. What sights, sounds, smells are present at the site.
3. If people are present at the site, tell their jobs.
4. Use plenty of illustrations. These can be photographs, pictures cut from old magazines or your own illustrations. Think of a good caption for each illustration.

A DAY IN THE LIFE OF _____

A DAY IN THE LIFE OF A TELEVISION NEWS REPORTER
By William Jaspersohn
Little, Brown and Company, 1981

This is a story about Dan Rea who loves the reporting life. His day starts with a walk to the mail room and a stop by the newsroom. The newsroom is always busy with typewriters clicking. A stop to see the news director and the producer is next. There are several hours of work before the news can be put on the air for viewing by the general public.

News Reporters

News reporters have many tasks to complete before they are ready to face the public. There are many people involved in the preparation of the day's news. There are many machines and technical problems involved in the production of a news show.

Directions

1. Choose a famous person in history.
    Examples: President Kennedy
                Prince Charles
                Christopher Columbus

2. List all the support people behind your famous person who helped make his/her accomplishments a success.

3. List any machines or technical advances that made his/her jobs easier.

4. Write a story with illustrations and use the title: A Day In the Life of _____. (Fill in the name of the famous person you have chosen). Use the same model as the book mentioned on this page.

A LETTER-WRITING PROJECT

The authors of FREE STUFF FOR KIDS have gathered information from many organizations and businesses about free materials they give away.

On each page of this book you are told:

> Where to write
>
> What to ask for
>
> Postage and/or
>
> > handling charges

Meadowbrook Press

Wayzata, MN 55391

FREE STUFF FOR KIDS

THE SECOND RAINBOW BOOK

By Pat Blakely, Barbara Haislet & Judith Hentges

Compile A State or Community "Free Stuff" Book

1. Determine the kinds of materials you want to include. (Print, nonprint, all free, some with small charges, specific subject areas, materials for older or younger children).

2. Analyze the major subject areas you want to include. What organizations or businesses deal with these subjects? Both the yellow pages and the lists of organizations in the almanac can help here.

3. Compose a letter asking about the availability of free materials and procedure(s) for obtaining the materials. Ask for samples of the materials to examine.

4. Compile your data in booklet form. Be sure to include all necessary information your reader will need to have to obtain the material.

A RESEARCH MODEL ON CAUSES AND EFFECTS

Greenwillow Books 1984

JUNK FOOD— WHAT IT IS, WHAT IT DOES

Judith S. Seixas
Pictures by TOM HUFFMAN

Most people know that junk food is not healthful. However, junk food is eaten more by people than almost any other kind of food.

List reasons why (causes) people eat junk food.

_____

_____

_____

_____

_____

_____

What effects will be noticed from eating too much junk food?

_____

_____

_____

The author of ALCOHOL— WHAT IT IS, WHAT IT DOES now provides another informative, easy to read and understand manual on a vitally important subject. Tailored for the audience that needs it most, here are the facts they should know on what junk food is and why it is bad for them.

Select a topic for research and report on the topic by giving as many causes and effects of of the topic as you can.

Possible Topic

Television: What It Is
            What It Does

Research what caused television to become such an important part of our lives.
Research the effects (what it does) of television on different parts of the population.

Other Possible Topics

Inflation: What It Is (Causes)
            What It Does (Effects)
Drugs: What They Are, What They Do

THE PEOPLE'S ALMANAC PRESENTS The Book of Predictions

BY DAVID WALLECHINSKY AMY WALLACE AND IRVING WALLACE

William Morrow Publishers, 1980

IS IT POSSIBLE TO PREDICT THE FUTURE?

These people would say yes!
    Business Analyst
    Demographer
    Physician
    Wall Street Analyst

Study the predictions below. Some were made by experts in their fields. Others were made by psychics. Can you tell which is which?

Select one prediction for research. From your research gather evidence to *support or deny the validity of the prediction.*

If possible, research one social aspect of your community. Predict future trends. Demonstrate with a graph. Example:
    Future building trends
    Size of school population
    Most popular means of
        transportation
    New businesses

Predictions

1998   The track record for the mile is 3 min. 32 sec.

1999   A computer makes an original scientific discovery and its program is nominated for a Nobel Prize.

2000   Areas of Texas and California split off to form new states. Wrist telephones are popular. Artificial eyesight is invented for blind people.

2003   After a U. S. stock market crash and major depression, the United States ceases to be a great power.

2010   All Persian Gulf countries run out of oil.

2012   If caught in the early stages, every kind of cancer is now curable.

2020   International terrorists, employing nuclear weapons, destroy a major world capital. This leads to police repression, which in turn leads to a worldwide disarmament conference. As a result, nuclear-weapon systems are scrapped.

2040   A democratic United States of the World is established.

GREAT MISTAKES!

"THE EARTH IS FLAT"—AND OTHER

GREAT MISTAKES

By Laurence Pringle
Illustrated by Steve Miller
William Morrow 1984

In this book Laurence Pringle has collected some of the greatest mistakes made by people throughout history. At the same time he gives basic reasons why people make mistakes.

They are:

1. Lack of knowledge
2. Ignoring the facts
3. Taking a risk

The mistakes in this book range from constructing a skyscraper with windows that pop out in a strong wind to the sinking of the Titanic.

Your Book of Great Mistakes

1. Interview family, teachers and friends about the greatest mistake each has made. Try to determine the reason for the mistake and include this in each account.

2. Compile a book about these great mistakes.

3. Illustrate your book if possible.

4. Your book should be one of the most read books in your school!

BIOGRAPHY REPORT

Subject's Name _____

Complete this questionnaire as if you *were* the subject!

1. If the Pied Piper of Hamelin asked me for money to rid our town of rats, I would:
   A. give him money gladly
   B. work on a committee to raise the money
   C. tell him "The more rats the better"
   D. say it's not my problem.

2. My favorite books are:
   A. fantasy tales
   B. adventure tales
   C. factual information
   D. sports stories

3. I feel it is best in any situation:
   A. to plan for it
   B. to dream about it
   C. to wait and see what happens
   D. to take immediate action

4. If I have a problem I prefer:
   A. to solve it myself
   B. individual counseling
   C. group counseling
   D. to ignore it

5. I would choose for a pet:
   A. a dog
   B. a cat
   C. a snake
   D. an exotic bird

6. I am most efficient in:
   A. planning
   B. predicting from scientific data
   C. discerning the moods of others
   D. using intuition as my guide

7. I remember best:
   A. how to perform a motor skill
   B. names
   C. faces
   D. statistics

8. My best subject in school is/was:
   A. speech
   B. philosophy
   C. math
   D. reading

9. I show my feelings:
   A. not at all
   B. easily
   C. in poetry, art or drama
   D. only when absolutely necessary

10. My opinion of Sidney Carton in <u>A Tale of Two Cities</u> is that:
    A. he was noble
    B. he was misguided
    C. he was stupid
    D. he was too drunk to know what he was doing

TURNING POINTS!

In more than a hundred surprising revealing and entertaining tales, the reader relives the creative experiences of history's most important innovators. In a trip behind the scenes we learn about:

The Accident That Created Rayon

The Visions That Propelled Nat
    Turner To His Fateful
    Rebellion

The Warm Bath That Led To
    Archimedes' Famous
    Mathematical Principle

The Writing Contest That Led To
    Mary Shelley's Frankenstein

The Supernatural Incident That
    Led Hitler To Power

The Conversation That Led
    Howard Maxim To Develop
    The Maxim Machine Gun

Brainstorms & Thunderbolts

How Creative Genius Works

Carol Orsag Madigan & Ann Elwood

Macmillan Publishing Company

New York 1983

Your Research Product

A BOOK ON TURNING POINTS IN ? ? ?

<u>What to do:</u>

1. Select a field of human endeavor of great interest to you.

2. Compile an extensive list of people who have made significant contributions to that field.

3. Locate biographical references. Read briefly about those on your list.

4. Select eight to twelve of those who most fascinate you. Research each life giving particular attention to TURNING POINTS which led to later significant achievement.

5. Tell about each turning point in story form. Illustrate with photos, slides or sketches, if possible.

Possible Topics

Turning points in the lives of scientists, military leaders, governmental leaders, inventors, artists, musicians, dancers, writers, poets, sports figures, labor leaders, journalists.

SETTING CRITERIA FOR A COLLECTIVE BIOGRAPHY

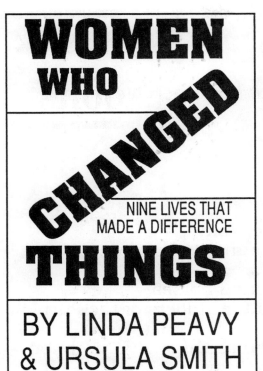

WOMEN WHO CHANGED THINGS is a collective biography of the lives of nine women. In selecting women for inclusion in this book the authors set the following exacting criteria:

THE WOMEN CHOSEN

1. Must have demonstrably changed the lives of others.
2. Must represent broad ethnic makeup and regional differences.
3. Must have written documentation of lives and achievements.
4. Must represent a wide variety of fields of endeavor.
5. Must have lived between 1880 and 1930.

Your Collective Biography

1. Select an area of focus.
   Ideas:
      a. the greatest problem solved by _____
      b. decisions that changed lives.
      c. turning points (in the lives of the great)
      d. early failure-late success
2. Establish written criteria for those who will be included in your book.
3. Research the lives of the people you choose to write about.
4. Write the accounts of these lives with particular attention to your area of focus.
5. Share your manuscript with your class, with your school, with your community; perhaps in the form of a weekly newspaper column.

Starter Ideas

Women Who Ruled
Women Who Influenced Others
Women Freedom Fighters

Women Who Cared
Women in Medicine
Women Who Made a Difference

WOMEN WHO CHANGED THINGS is published by Charles Scribner's Sons. 1983.

RESEARCHING PERSONALITIES

The Bio-Poem

A bio-poem is one way to briefly tell about someone's life.

Here is an example:

TOM MIX

Tom
Tall, thin, lanky, beardless,
Felt like a brother to his horse, Tony.
Who cared deeply about his country's freedom,
Who felt confident on a horse,
Who needed to live his life around horses,
Who gave audiences enjoyment in "Riders of the Purple Sage"
Who feared he might do the wrong thing at a reception given for him by the Lord Mayor of London
Who wished to see no more wars like those he fought in,
Resident of Hollywood, California.

Now try one of your own. Select a person whose biography you have read and follow the pattern given below.

Line 1 - Name _____

Line 2 - Four traits _____

Line 3 - Related to _____

Line 4 - Who cares deeply about _____

Line 5 - Who feels _____

Line 6 - Who needs _____

Line 7 - Who gives _____

Line 8 - Who fears _____

Line 9 - Who would like to see _____

Line 10- Resident of _____

YOU CAN BUILD A

BETTER MOUSETRAP

Discover:
Getting started in inventing tools for
    the inventor's workshop
Keeping notebooks (how to)
Planning procedures
Naming your invention
Patents
Marketing your invention
Great invention stories

Research the beginnings of one or
more inventions detailed in this
book.

Predict what would happen if this
invention were not now a part of our
lives.

Workman Publishing Co. 1985

Inventing Rube Goldberg Style

Use any six action components to create an imaginative Rube Goldberg style sequential design invention for these ideas:

Automatic Fanning Machine For Hot Days

Bedroom Burglar Alarm

Remote Control TV Channel Changer

Around the Block Dog Walker

Garbage Disposal Device

Your Own Invention Idea

A Better Mousetrap

Mouse comes out of hiding for submarine sandwich (bait) left on counter. Mouse follows line of bread crumbs. Mouse walks into path of fan and is blown across counter... into false teeth. Teeth clamp shut to hold mouse... also pulling a string... which tilts water can to drown mouse.

 CAT
 ICE CUBES
 CHAMPAGNE
 MATCHES
 CUCKOO CLOCK
 PIGEON

 CANNON
 HORN
 SPRINGBOARD
 BUCKET
 SAW
 TEA KETTLE

 BALLOON
 WEIGHT
 CANDLE
 FROG
 MAGNET
 UMBRELLA

BECOME AN INVENTOR
APPLY FLEXIBLE THINKING

Inventors look at things that people need and by bringing elements together in new ways, find ways to meet these needs. Look at the items pictured below. Combine these items, using as many as you can to invent:

Something that will be very useful in your classroom or school.

46

A HOW-THEY-DO-IT PATTERN

A Clothing Report

Share CHARLIE NEEDS A CLOAK by Tomie dePaola, (Prentice Hall, 1973). Use story strips to sequence the steps in which the sheep's wool becomes Charlie's cloak. Use the steps in a pattern poem similar to the one below which gives the steps in turning the cotton plant into a wearable garment.

COTTON
I WONDER WHY THEY....
    Prepare the soil
    Plant the seeds
    Cultivate the earth
    Spray the crops
    Pick the cotton
    Remove the fibers
    Bale the lint
    Truck the bales
    Clean the cotton
    Spin the thread
    Weave the yarn
    Dye the cloth
    Cut and sew
When we could wear *wool*
    instead!

WOOL
I WONDER WHY THEY...

_____

_____

_____

_____

_____

_____

_____

_____

_____

When we could wear _____
    instead!

A HOW-TO MODEL

HOW I TRAINED MY COLT
By Sandy Rabinowitz
Doubleday, 1980

This is a story about a young girl who trains her colt named Sunny. The book begins with the birth of the colt. The young girl begins working with the animal almost immediately. The girl said, "I wanted to ride him when he grew up. So he had to learn to obey me. He was only two days old. I was bigger and stronger than he was. It was time for Sunny's first lesson."

This book takes the reader from the time the colt was born until he was trained for riding. Each step of the training is carefully described.

Animal Training

Almost any animal can be trained to perform in some way.
Training procedures differ for each animal.
The library has many books on animal training.
Some circus performers train animals.
Some animal trainers work for large zoos.
Obedience schools train animals also.

Creative Reporting

1. Check several resources for information regarding the training of one type of animal.

2. Provide pictures or drawings of the animal that you have chosen.

3. Using the model above develop an instruction manual for training your animal.

4. Decide where the best place would be for the training to take place.

5. Be sure to mention in your story what you hope to accomplish with this training.

Possible choices

hamster	guinea pig	rabbit
elephant	goldfish	monkey
dog	bird	

HOW TO DIG A HOLE
TO THE OTHER SIDE OF THE WORLD

HOW TO DIG A HOLE TO THE OTHER SIDE OF THE WORLD
By Faith McNulty
Harper & Row, 1979

One would have to dig 8,000 miles to reach the other side of the earth. Use a shovel and start digging in a soft place. Loam is the first layer of the earth, which is made of tiny bits of rock mixed with many other things such as plants and worms that died and rotted long ago. In your dig you may hit boiling water or steam that comes from the center of the earth. Stay out of the geysers which may carry you to the surface and shoot you into the air. Find out what causes volcanoes as you journey through this book.

Use this model to prepare a booklet of your journey to the bottom of the ocean. Tell about the animals you might meet along the way to the bottom. What gear would you use to get down to the bottom of the of the ocean? Tell the dangers of the ocean as they did in this book.

<u>What to do:</u>

1. Read all factual material about the ocean.

2. You are the main character so write in the first person (I).

3. Include charts and illustrations in your booklet.

THINGS TO DO WITH WATER

THINGS TO DO WITH WATER
By Illa Podendorf
Childrens Press, 1971

As a liquid, water can be made into many different shapes— a circle, a square, etc. By using food colors water can virtually become any color— red, blue, or yellow. By mixing two different colors the water can create a new color such as purple, mixed from red and blue. Water can be evaporated into the air. Experiments with water can be fun and unpredictable. Try these simple experiments in your home. Do you get the same results?

Using this as a model try experimenting with other objects and record the results.

Possible objects to experiment with

ice	wood
air	magnets
sugar	play-doh
clay	dirt
sand	

<u>What to do:</u>

1. Pick an object to experiment with.

2. Do four experiments as in the book.

3. Describe the experiment in your book.

4. Put the results of your experiment after the explanation.

HOW A HOUSE HAPPENS

HOW A HOUSE HAPPENS
By Jan Adkins
Walker and Company, 1972

When building a house one must go through certain steps. One must decide what kind of house is needed (how big, where the rooms should be placed, how many doors and windows, etc.). When a site is picked for the house, the architect can draw up a blueprint or a plan of the house. After the blueprint is finished the contractor and the workmen can start building the house. This book will take you plank by plank through building a house, explaining plumbing and electrical processes and much more.

Using this model research the way other things are made.

Possible items to research:

       Automobile assembly line

       How a computer is built

<u>What to do:</u>

1.   Research your subject.

2.   Write a step by step description of the process, the people who work with developing the item and the parts used.

3.   Include diagrams.

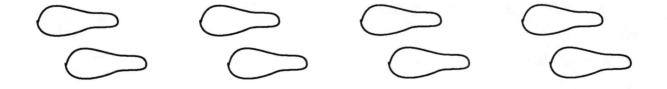

VITAMINS—
WHAT THEY ARE,
WHAT THEY DO

Vitamins—
What They Are,
What They Do

By JUDITH S. SEIXAS
Illustrated by Tom Huffman

With the same clarity and straightforward presentation that distinguished her highly regarded books on alcohol and tobacco, Judith S. Seixas introduces young readers to vitamins. What vitamins are, how they were discovered, how they work, and whether or not they are safe are some of the topics covered. A complex subject at once made understandable and interesting. Included are a vitamin chart and a true/false test for readers.
Greenwillow Books, 1986.

Following the pattern of this informational book, select another topic and tell WHAT IT IS and WHAT IT DOES.

Include in your illustrated book:

    What it is.

    How it was discovered or invented.

    How it works.

    How safe it is.

    A chart or graph.

    Diagrams as needed.

    A quiz for your reader at the end of the book.

RE/USES

RE/USES

2133 Ways to RECYCLE and REUSE the Things You Ordinarily Throw Away

CAROLYN JABS

Line drawings by Robert Duffek
Crown Publishers, Inc. 1982

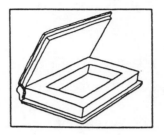

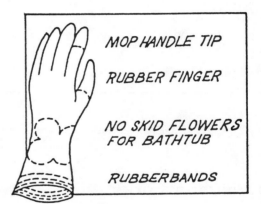

MOP HANDLE TIP

RUBBER FINGER

NO SKID FLOWERS FOR BATHTUB

RUBBER BANDS

RE-USES is a book about being smart by using what you already have.

It speaks to beating the high cost of living by making more and buying less.

RE-USES recognizes that few people individually can use all the trash they produce. It helps you find out who can use your discards...and perhaps pay you for them.

Find out!
What is wasted or thrown away each day in your school?

How could it be used?

What to do:

1. Identify sources of waste material and possible uses of this material.

2. Make a plan for manufacturing a useful product.

3. Research sources of loans for start up money.

4. Plan how to produce, package, and market the product.

5. Investigate government regulations for small businesses.

6. Make your product!

PRODUCTS REQUIRING FLEXIBLE THINKING
Recycle Your School!!!

From Bottle Caps You Can Make

Shoe Scraper

Games

Tambourine

Washers

Fish Scale Scraper

Buttons

From Plastic Meal or Serving Trays You Can Make

Paper Plates

Drip Catchers

Stencil Patterns

Shoe Cushions

Insulation For Shoes

Artist Palette

Anti Book Slipper

Anti Rug Slipper

From Old Forks You Can Make

Mini Rakes

Decorator Forks

Money Fork

Bracelet

What Could You Do With

Old Records

Old Newspapers

Toothpaste Tubes

Pencil Shavings

Waste Paper

Orange Peels

How will you manufacture your product?

Where can you get a loan for "start up" money?

How will you package, market and sell your product?

What business regulations will you need to follow?

SO YOU DON'T LIKE TO WRITE!

Try: The Newspaper Clipping Report

Step One:
Select a topic. This can be on a current event or a general topic.

Here are topics to think about.

Aircraft	New Ideas
Business	Olympic Games
Conservation	Propaganda
Disasters	Quasars
Earth-Our-Home	Record-Setting Events
Funny Happenings	Space
Great Performances	Technology
Human Interest Stories	Unusual Events
Interesting People	Victories
Joyful Moments	Water
Keepers of Freedom	X-Rays and Other Medical Miracles
Law and Order	
Misunderstandings	Youthful Accomplishments
	Zealots

NEWSPAPER CLIPPING REPORT continued

Step Two:

Make a list of all the possible things you might look for and clip as you begin your report.

Here are some topic ideas to get your thinking started.

KEEPERS OF FREEDOM!

How quickly can you find these in a newspaper— add other items

1. A picture that symbolizes freedom
2. A patriotic headline
3. An article about loss of freedom
4. An event that could take place only in a free society
5. A statement concerning freedom of speech
6. A controversial topic
7. The name of one who can do something about injustice
8. The name or picture of a female leader
9.
10.
11.
12.
13.
14.
15.
16.
17.
18.
19.
20.

CONSERVATION

Find a picture, name or article about these— add other items

1. A natural resource that is not wildlife
2. A major water source
3. Something that needs to be conserved
4. A product good for the environment
5. Good advice for saving something
6. Someone to write to about a conservation problem
7. Something currently being rehabilitated
8.
9.
10.
11.
12.
13.
14.
15.

TECHNOLOGY

Find a picture, name or article about these— add other items

1. An energy producer
2. Something a computer expert might use
3. An invention to use in your home
4. An industry that might pollute
5. An example of mass transportation
6. Someone to write about an environmental concern
7. A product that might pollute
8. Someone's opinion of technology
9. A technological job opening
10. Technology in the kitchen
11. Third world technology
12.
13.
14.
15.

Putting it all together!

Watch your newspaper for ads, photographs, cartoons and features related to the subject you choose.

Begin clipping!

Sort your clippings into major subject headings...this can be by date or by type of feature or other headings you choose.

Display for others to see:
in a book
on the bulletin board
or other display

REPORTING

WITH A

CAMERA,

PAINTS AND

PENCIL

THE ILLUSTRATED OR PHOTOGRAPHIC ESSAY

DAKOTA DUGOUT by Ann Turner, illustrated by Ronald Himler (MacMillan, 1985) is an illustrated account of a young married couple building and living in their first home on the prairie, a dugout. The land is shown as the seasons change with both the joy and hardships of nature being experienced.

Use your camera or your sketchpad to record in visual form a series of happenings or events. This means of recording information is particularly effective in showing changes in nature. For example, if you select a place you often see (perhaps your back yard) and begin a series of photos you can show changes in nature and seasons very effectively.

THE ILLUSTRATED DICTIONARY

Select a topic. For each letter of the alphabet list one word that is related to the topic in some way. Each page in the alphabet book on your topic will illustrate one letter of the alphabet, HOWEVER, note the example at the bottom of the page! A IS NOT FOR ALLIGATOR. S is for alligator because alligators have sharp teeth. Have fun thinking of letters for each of your words. Perhaps you can fool your reader.

A _____   N _____

B _____   O _____

C _____   P _____

D _____   Q _____

E _____   R _____

F _____   S alligator (sharp teeth) _____

G _____   T _____

H _____   U _____

I _____   V _____

J _____   W _____

K _____   X _____

L _____   Y _____

M _____   Z _____

**S is for alligator
Why?**

Alligators have
sharp teeth!

OBSERVING AN ANIMAL

KITTEN CAN . . .
By Bruce McMillan
Lothrop, Lee, & Shepard, 1984

This book is a book full of verbs. The verbs describe the actions of a kitten. The pictures also tell the story of what the kitten does. This is one active animal. It sniffs, climbs, stalks, and springs.

<u>Kittens are very active animals.</u>

There are many other animals that are active and there are some animals that are not as active.
The library has many books about animals.
Observation of an animal can also be useful in developing a story about an animal.

<u>Things to search for:</u>

How the animal moves.
How the animal eats.
How the animal plays.
How the animal uses its senses.
Any other interesting traits the animal possesses.

<u>Example:</u> "Kitten can stare, squeeze, stretch, and scratch."

<u>What to do:</u>

1. Check several sources for information regarding the animal of your choice.

2. List all the action verbs you can find that pertain to your animal.

3. Using the model above, create a story about an animal and be sure to provide illustrations. (Replace the word kitten with the name of your animal).

THE PICTORIAL JOURNAL

Here is the story of one family facing all of the dangers and hardships in moving west. Accurate information, cartoon-style illustrations and a first person narrative make this a most exciting real-life tale.

What event from history will you select to research?

From whose viewpoint will you tell the event?

What will happen to your narrator at the end of your story?

Note the importance of details in recreating a particular time or place. What details will be important to your story?

Remember, a picture can tell the story! Your captions under each picture should add to the story (not tell what is in the picture).

GOING WEST

STORY BY
Martin WADDELL

PICTURES BY
Philippe DUPASQUIER

Ma

Kate

Peter

Pa

Louisa

© 1984

Harper & Row, Publishers

Possible Journeys For Research

Traveling to the new world with Columbus

A Jewish family escaping from Germany in 1939

The first astronauts to travel to the moon

Traveling to China with Marco Polo, or traveling with a famous explorer

Life on the Santa Fe Trail or the Oregon Trail

Riding a bicycle across the United States or Canada

Traveling down the Mississippi River

RESEARCHING COMMUNITY CHURCHES

Ashley Wolff, in writing and illustrating THE BELLS OF LONDON, chose one small part of that large, busy city to tell about in pictures and verse. For each church featured in the book there is a rhyming couplet.

"Oranges and lemons,
Say the bells of St. Clements."

Play with words!

What might these bells sing?

St. Johns

St. Annes

St. Martins

Old Bailey

Shoreditch

Stepney

Bow

St. Peters

St. Giles

White Chapel

St. Margarets

Aldgate

St. Catherines

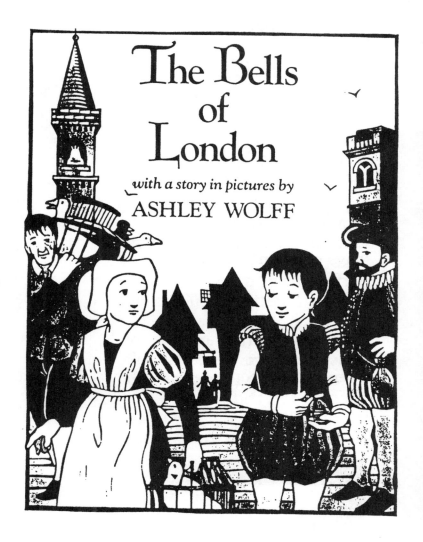

Dodd Mead, 1985

1. How many churches in your community have bells?

2. Make a list of the churches and their locations.

3. Write to each church for a picture of the church (or take pictures of those nearest you).

4. Compose a rhyming couplet telling of what the bells of each church might sing.

5. Put your work in booklet form to share with others.

THE OPTICAL ILLUSION BOOK

SEYMOUR SIMON
Illustrated with drawings and photographs

Praised as "fascinating" (*Horn Book*) and "extraordinary" (*Appraisal*), this classic book on optical illusions is now in paperback! Readers will discover: why two lines can look uneven when both are really the same length; how perspective creates three-dimensional images; the ways color and brightness influence perception; how artists use illusions to create new vistas. Over 80 illustrations and many fun visual experiments let readers see how and why these illusions work. Proving that you can't always believe what you see, this book is sure to open young people's eyes.
Morrow Junior Books 1984

FOOLING FOLKS

WITH

PHOTOGRAPHS

This book shows that even though we might all look at the same scene or picture, we do not necessarily see the same thing.

Use this idea as a basis for a photographic or a multi-picture research project. You can use a series of unrelated photographs or you might want to use photos all on one topic.

Each photo you include can be captioned to ask the viewer for a response. For example: you might show part of an object and ask the viewer to identify the object.

or

You might show people engaged in an unusual occupation or event and ask the reader what or why they are doing what they are doing. Explain the real reason on the next page!

or

Research the works of artists who are well known for the use of optical illusion in their paintings or drawings.

Study The Picture Books Of Mitsumasa Anno

In his books, ANNO'S JOURNEY, ANNO'S ITALY, ANNO'S BRITAIN and ANNO'S U.S.A., this artist uses many optical illusion tricks! Make a list of all those you find and share them with your friends.

or

Prepare a photographic display of as many optical illusions as you can find. These can be photographs you take or photographs you find in newspapers or magazines.

BLENDING

FACT

AND

FICTION

COMPARING CULTURES WITH FOLKTALES
The Emperor's New Clothes

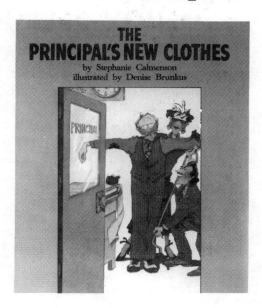

Stephanie Calmenson's funny book, THE PRINCIPAL'S NEW CLOTHES (Schloastic, 1989) tells the same story as the well-known tale by Hans Christian Andersen, THE EMPEROR'S NEW CLOTHES. Only the setting and main characters of the stories are different.

All folk tales reveal something about the country or culture from which they come. Use the chart below to compare your culture with that shown in a favorite tale.

CULTURE COMPARISON CHART

Title of Folktale _____

Elements of Culture		Folktale Culture	Your Culture
Most popular means of transportation			
Most popular medium of information			
Most popular music			
Most respected profession(s)			
Role of male ..	Active Passive?		
Role of female..	Involved Onlooker? Assertive? Submissive?		

This tale is set in _____ century _____ .
country

WRITER'S BLOCK

Written and illustrated by
MARSHA BAKER

Printed in USA

Copyright © 1984 by
Book Lures, Inc.

USING CARTOONS IN WRITING THE HOW-TO BOOK

In this example the author has used cartoons to explain how to start writing when you don't have any ideas. While the cartoons are humorous, good advice is found in the story. Use this idea to write an advice or a how-to book after carefully researching the topic you choose.

WRITER'S BLOCK IS ONE OF THE MOST DREADED DISEASES KNOWN TO MAN

HOWEVER, DO NOT DESPAIR! THE EXPERTS HAVE GOTTEN TOGETHER TO COME UP WITH A CURE FOR WRITER'S BLOCK.

DO YOU HAVE A LOT ON YOUR MIND?

I.M.Habit

TAKE A LOAD OFF.

RELAX! TAKE A WHOLE WEEK OFF

DON'T BE CHAINED TO HABIT

STRETCH YOUR MIND! READ ABOUT NEW AND INTERESTING THINGS

LET YOUR IMAGINATION RUN WILD

AFTER THIS WRITER'S BLOCK WILL BE GONE AND YOU WILL BE WRITING ONCE AGAIN!

THE RIDDLE POEM

ANIMAL HABITATS
The Ten Fact Riddle Poem

Here is a poem about a woodland creature that contains ten facts.
The name of the creature is given in the last line of the poem. Use
this poem as a model. Find interesting information about another
woodland creature and include the facts you find in a riddle poem.

WHAT IS IT ???

This riddle poem, if you're a whiz,
Will tell you what this creature is.

How big is it do you suppose?
32 inches from its tail to its nose?

It has long legs and sharp, sharp claws.
Enough to give a hunter pause.

A favorite food is fresh crayfish,
But frogs can make a tasty dish.

Its home is in a hollow tree,
Its coarse gray hair is hard to see.

Around its tail are black ring hoops,
It robs bird's nests and chicken coops.

If you don't guess this creature soon,
I'll tell you. . . it's a wild RACCOON.

The owl is an interesting forest
creature. There are many different
kinds of owls. Research one type of
owl and write a riddle poem about it
similar to the poem above.

A STORY REPORT

I MET A POLAR BEAR
By Selma and Pauline Boyd
Lothrop, Lee & Shepard, 1983

Here is a story model for reporting research on animal homes. On his way to school a boy meets a polar bear, an earthworm and an ant. In helping each to return to its natural home the boy is late to school.

1. What animals will you decide to meet on your way to school?
   Name four.

   a. _____   c. _____

   b. _____   d. _____

2. What is the natural home of each animal?

   a. _____   c. _____

   b. _____   d. _____

3. How will you help each animal return to its natural home?

   a. _____

   b. _____

   c. _____

   d. _____

4. Write and illustrate your story. Decide how to explain being late to your teacher.

5. Share your story with friends.

THE TRUTH ABOUT...

THE TRUTH ABOUT THE MOON by Clayton Bess (Houghton Mifflin, 1983) points up the contrasts between modern and traditional beliefs by combining current scientific knowledge and imaginative folklore.

This book can serve as an excellent model for reporting on the differences between mythological and factual explanations of nature.

Decide what topic you would like to tell the truth about!

What legends or stories exist about the topic?

Read and briefly summarize the legends. Locate factual information about the topic.

Write your book alternating pages of myth and factual explanation.
or
State a mythological explanation you have found for some aspect of nature and ask your reader whether it is fact or fiction. On the page that follows let your reader know the answer and give the scientific explanation for the event.

Possible Titles

The Truth About Tides　　　The Truth About Comets
The Truth About Weather　　The Truth About Roses
The Truth About Skunks　　 The Truth About _____

PROBLEM-SOLVING

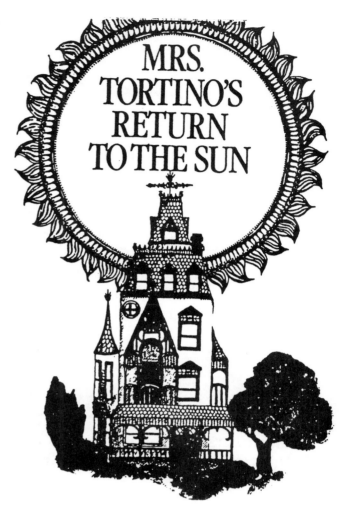

One way an author can tell about real-life problems is to present the problem in story form.

Mrs. Tortino lives in a tiny older home surrounded by tall new buildings. These buildings block out the sun and the busy street traffic pollutes the air. Even though her plants begin to die and her cat begins to wheeze, Mrs. Tortino refuses to move. Instead, she finds a unique way to get back sunshine and fresh air!

Create A Solution!

Write a story about a different problem (world hunger, unemployment, crime, noise pollution).

by Shirley and Pat Murphy
Lothrop, Lee & Shepard, 1980

What to do:

1. Read about the topic (problem) you have chosen.

2. List solutions suggested by others.

3. Decide on a main character and how this character is affected by the problem.

4. Plan your solution.

5. Write your story, solving the problem.

6. Illustrate your story if possible.

IF YOU LIVED...

How would your life be different if you lived in the country instead of the city or the city instead of the country? Alice and Martin Provensen's beautiful book TOWN AND COUNTRY (Harper Collins, 1987) will tell you. The tasks we do each day often depend on where we live. Try writing a story about a character who lives in a special place. Include in your story the jobs that person might have to do if he/she lived:

In a lighthouse	At the White House
In a weather station at the North Pole	In a firehouse
In a forest ranger's cabin	On a ranch
Other _____	

Decide:

1.   Who will be the main character in your story?

2.   What tasks will the character perform?

3.   Who will help the character?

4.   What problem will the character or the helper have?

5.   How will the problem be solved?

TAKE AN UNEXPECTED TRIP

MOUSEKIN TAKES A TRIP
Prentiss Hall, Inc., 1976
Story and pictures by Edna Miller

A white footed mouse is searching for food. He ventures into a camper trailer and the door shuts behind him. As he is munching on some food the trailer begins to move and mouse is on his way.

The trailer, pulled by a car, travels for a long time and when it stops, mouse prepares to escape. As the trailer door opens, mouse springs free and lands right in the middle of a desert.

The sights, sounds, and animals are all new to mouse. He is frightened and alone.

What did mouse see and hear?
What animals lived there?
How did mouse get home?

The story answers all of these questions.

Take an Unexpected Trip

Using the above model, take your reader on an unexpected trip through one of the fifty states. Make your story interesting by including the sights and sounds of the state as was done by the desert trip that mouse took.

Don't forget that the climate and topography are also important.

What to do:

1. Read as much as you can on the state you choose.
2. List all points of interest you want to use.
3. Place your locations in a logical order.
4. Choose a small animal as your main character.
5. Be sure to include how he accidentally took this trip.
6. Write your story taking your character to several sights and explain the climate it encounters.
7. Make the ending happy by returning the animal to it's home.
8. Use illustrations when possible.

KEEP A DIARY!

A MOUSE'S DIARY
By Michelle Cartlidge
Lothrop, Lee & Shepard Books, 1981

A mouse keeps a diary for a week telling of the activities he is involved in each day of the week.

Sunday

I went to the park with my father and mother and younger brother. We had a lovely picnic.

Monday

At ballet class today we pretended to be candles on a great big birthday cake.

Tuesday

After school my mother took us to the toy shop.

Using the format of this book, write a diary that a historical person might have kept based on facts you find in your research.

Possible Historical Figures

Paul Revere during Revolutionary War
George Washington when crossing the Delaware
Jim Bowie at the Alamo
Molly Pitcher during the Revolutionary War
Sacajawea guiding Lewis and Clark

What to do:

1. Read biographies and autobiographies of the person you have picked.
2. Check history books.
3. Compile information in diary form as if you were the historical person (use first person "I").

CONTRASTING LIFESTYLES

TOBY IN THE COUNTRY, TOBY IN THE CITY
By Maxine Zohn Bozzo
Greenwillow Books, 1982

In this book two boys named Toby lead practically the same lives, except one boy lives in the city and the other boy lives in the country. Toby in the country lives on a farm while Toby in the city lives in an apartment. The street in front of Toby's house in the country is a gravel road bordered with trees. The street in front of Toby's apartment in the city is a busy intersection with a few trees. Toby in the country plays games in the woods with his friends. Toby in the city plays hopscotch on the busy sidewalk with his friends. The two boys do many of the same things but in different ways because life in the city is different from life in the country.

Use this model to compare and contrast two subjects. Illustrations will be necessary for this project.

Possible items to compare and contrast

The Indians and the Pilgrims

Two types of dinosaurs

A child in France or Spain to a child in U. S.

What To Do:

1. Decide on the two subjects.

2. Research the subjects in the library, in an encyclopedia, a social studies book, or a specialty book about your subject.

3. After gathering information needed, write and illustrate your book.

EDIBLE ORIGINS

RESEARCHING THE SOURCE OF FOODS WE EAT

PANCAKE PIE
By SVEN NORDQVIST
Morrow Junior Books, 1985.

Wily Farmer Festus and his exuberant cat, Mercury, like to make a good thing even better. Three times a year they sit down to a mouth-watering pancake pie and celebrate Mercury's birthday. But one birthday morning, absolutely nothing goes right. Before he can bake the pie, Festus has to fish a key from the bottom of a deep well, wade through a puddle of broken eggs, and outwit an angry bull with fast cat Mercury as matador. With luck, pluck, and wild invention, Festus and Mercury get over, under, and around all obstacles to have their best birthday celebration ever!

PANCAKE PIE is a great spoof on finding and using all of the ingredients found in a birthday pie.

This same idea can be used in weaving factual information into a humorous story about securing the ingredients in any recipe!

Remember, the primary source of all foods is the SUN.

Select a recipe. Develop a chart showing how all the ingredients can be traced back to the sun. Use this information in developing a humorous story about preparing this recipe. Decide WHY this recipe is being prepared (what is the important event?). WHO is the recipe being prepared for? WHEN will the dish be served? WHERE will it be served? WHAT will happen during the finding of the ingredients?

Remember: Every story has
        characters
        setting
        problem
        solution

An Alternate Foods Research Project

The President of the United States has just informed you that he or she has selected your home as the typical home in your state and plans to come to dinner.

Plan a menu of the dinner you will serve the President. You may only use foods raised or grown in your state. You may only use ingredients raised or grown in your state.

What will you serve the president?

DESCRIBING WHAT A THING IS NOT!

THE MAN WHOSE NAME WAS NOT THOMAS
By M. Jean Craig
Doubleday and Company, Inc. 1981

"The man whose name was not Thomas or Richard either had to earn a living, just as most men do. He was not a blacksmith or a carpenter. He did not weave cloth or mend shoes. He was not a farmer or a bricklayer or a fisherman. He was something else."

Through the following pages this man is described, but not by what he is, but by what he is not.

Use this model to describe an animal.

What to do:

1. Decide on an animal.

2. Read about this animal and compare it to other animals.

3. Describe what it is by what it is not and can not do.

4. Place your information in a logical order.

SAMPLE:

Rover was not a cat. He was not a rabbit either. He was not a turtle, or an ant or a spider. He was not a monkey or rooster or duck. In fact, he was not even a bear. No he was called something else.

Continue to describe your animal by what he does not do, where he does not live, what he does not eat, what he does not like, etc.

LOOKING AT HISTORY THROUGH OTHER EYES

Suppose that the bulk mail rates were drastically reduced and all bulk mail was released on the same day. Should this happen, the total weight would cause our entire civilization to collapse.

David Macaulay begins MOTEL OF THE MYSTERIES with this assumption.

The book opens in the year 7000 A. D. A group of archaeologists are unearthing the North American civilization of the 1990s. One of the first things found is a motel (which is assumed to be a tomb).

1. What significance might the scientists give to:
    A television set?   A telephone?   A shower cap?
    A Do Not Disturb sign?   A drain stopper?

2. Use this same idea to report on a current place or event through the eyes of one from another civilization. Here are some ideas to get you started.

<u>How Would</u>   <u>View</u>
Orville and Wilber Wright   A modern airport
Alexander the Great   A guided missle site
Shakespeare   A word processing lab
Florence Nightengale   An intensive care unit
Marconi   A television studio

THE LITTLE WORM BOOK

Janet & Allan Ahlberg

THE VIKING PRESS   NEW YORK

THE COMMON WORM

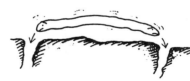

All good worms have a beginning, a middle and an end.

Worms with two beginnings, a middle and no end are apt to injure themselves.

Worms with two ends, a middle and no beginning get bored.

4. WORMS IN WARTIME
During the final stages of World War Two special teams of worms were trained to carry secret messages behind enemy lines.

1.
2.
3. RUN FOR IT

Viking Press, 1979

In this spoof on the formal research paper, the Ahlbergs have presented a topic in five chapters. *The topic is worms!*

They have called their paper
THE LITTLE WORM BOOK
Contents:

Chapter One: The Common Worm
Chapter Two: You And Your Worm
Chapter Three: Worms Around The World
Chapter Four: A Short History Of The Worm
Chapter Five: Worms Of Character

Select a topic of interest to you. Read this model carefully. Note how the authors make the absurd seem plausible!

What chapters might you have on your topic? Illustrations will help in your spoof as they do in the Ahlberg's book!

THE TIN-POT FOREIGN GENERAL AND THE OLD IRON WOMAN
A stunning anti-war statement
by Raymond Briggs illustrated in full color and black and white by the author

Raymond Briggs, author of the critically acclaimed book, WHEN THE WIND BLOWS, has written another provocative anti-war statement. In both art and text, this book evokes the mania, futility, and senseless horrors of war. This particular story is about the Falkland Islands War, but the statement Mr. Briggs makes is much more far-reaching and concerns the broader ramifications of man's inhumanity to man as exercised in the deadliest power game of all—WAR!

History As Satire
Satire: An artistic work that attacks human vice or foolishness with irony, derision or wit.

In this satire the author chooses a recent historical event, the Falkland Islands War and through gross exaggeration shows the foolishness of this or any other conflict between human beings.
1. Study Briggs' technique as demonstrated in this work.
2. Select another incident from recent or past history.
3. Decide how you can exaggerate the incident to present your message.

Examples

Suppose Chicken Little were concerned with nuclear fallout.

What if the country mouse visited the city mouse at the White House?

How would JACK AND THE BEANSTALK be different if Jack's mother received an allotment for NOT growing beans?

Suppose the THREE BILLY GOATS GRUFF were trying to cross the Great Wall of China.

THE TIN POT FOREIGN GENERAL AND THE OLD IRON WOMAN is published by Little-Brown Pub., 1985.

RECORD
BOOKS

82

A BOOK OF AVERAGES

Here is a book about things that *usually* happen each day in the United States. From this book you can discover:

How many American teenagers receive allowances.

How much the average American family watches television.

How many Americans order hamburgers, steaks or other items as their favorite restaurant food and hundreds of other facts.

The "Average American" Book

How happy we are • How honest we are • Our musical tastes • How often we go to McDonalds • How much we drink • How much television our kids watch •

WHAT THE LATEST SURVEYS, POLLS AND LIFESTYLE STUDIES TELL US ABOUT THE NOT VERY AVERAGE AMERICAN PEOPLE

Compiled and Edited
Barry Tarshis

Atheneum, 1979

A Class Project

In One Day At _____ School

Compile a book of statistics about your school. It is sure to be a best seller! Gather statistics from the library, office, nurse, custodian, other classrooms, and bus drivers. Keep records for two weeks and average your figures to arrive at a statistic. Brainstorm with friends concerning items to research. Here are starters.

1. How many pencils are sharpened in your school each day?
2. How many students (or teachers) are late each day?
3. How many lunches are served?
4. How many band-aids are used?
   Keep going!

DECISION MAKING

DAVID FROST'S BOOK OF THE WORLD'S WORST ~~DECISIONS~~ DESISIONS

by David Frost and Michael Deakin
illustrated by Arnie Levin

Here is a collection of truly appalling decisions!
Notable bad decisions covered include:

- the famous firm that turned down the patent for the typewriter, safe in the knowledge that "No mere machine can replace an honest and reliable clerk."

- the German technical institute that refused admittance to young Albert Einstein because "he showed no promise."

- the literature professor who gave a 0 in composition to one of his pupils - Emile Zola.

- the twenty-one publishers who turned down M. A. S. H.

Your Project

The worst decisions of:

> Our Town
> Our School
> Our Class

1. Select the group you want to survey. Here is a collection of truly appalling decisions!

2. Consider convincing arguments to convince those you interview to share their worst decisions for publication.

3. Compile and categorize your data.

4. Write your book!

STRANGE FACTS

WOULD YOU BELIEVE THIS, TOO?
More Useless Information You Can't Afford To Be Without
By Deidre Sanders
Illustrated by Joyce Behr
Sterling Publishing Co., Inc. 1976

WOULD YOU BELIEVE THIS, TOO? is a collection of strange facts. This book is filled with information about people, plants, animals, history, science, literature, business, industry, agriculture, and sports.

> "Scaled up to size and speed, the common house spider could give a world champion sprinter eight seconds start in a 100-meter race and still beat him."

A fact is information that is really true. Some facts are so strange that they are hard to believe.

Sometimes people believe information that is not true. These beliefs or customs are called superstitions. Sometimes these sayings are also called wive's tales.

Use this model as a way of reporting research about superstitions, old sayings, and wive's tales.

<u>What to do:</u>
1.   Collect as many sayings, superstitions, and old wive's tales as you can find.
2.   Construct a book. Each page should contain one or two sayings.
3.   Tell whether the statement is true or false.
4.   Illustrate the pages and design a cover for your book.
5.   Give your book a title.

Where To Search

Interview as many people as possible. Most people have heard a number of superstitions and will be happy to share them with you.

THE BIG BOOK OF ANIMAL RECORDS

THE BIG BOOK OF ANIMAL RECORDS
written and illustrated by Annette
Tison and Talus Taylor
An animal record book.

From the pygmy shrew weighing less than an ounce to the great blue whale, here are all kinds of animals and facts about which is the largest, the smallest, the fastest, the slowest, and, of course, the strangest and most unusual. Annette Tison, a young French artist and naturalist, and Talus Taylor, an artist and former biology teacher, have collaborated on several popular children's books. For THE BIG BOOK OF ANIMAL RECORDS, they worked on the text and illustrations for two years to convey the information strikingly, accurately, and also humorously.

Here are all kinds of records set by all kinds of animals! As you read this book, note the kinds of records cited.

To Write Your Book

1. Select a topic. The Big Book of (Insect) (Fish) (Mammal) (Reptile) Records.

2. Decide on the records you will include. List several here.

    a. The fastest _____

    b. The oldest _____

    c. The _____ which sleeps the longest.

    d. The _____ with the most _____ .

    e. _____
3. Research the answers to your questions. Each question and answer can be an illustrated page in your book.

THE BIG BOOK OF ANIMAL RECORDS is published by Grosset & Dunlap, 1985.

AMAZING ACHIEVEMENTS

THE GUINNESS BOOK OF AMAZING ACHIEVEMENTS
By Norris and Ross McWhirter
Sterling Publishing Co., 1974

In THE GUINNESS BOOK OF AMAZING ACHIEVEMENTS many amazing things that people have done are recorded. You can read about everything from the longest mustache ever grown to the person with the strongest teeth in the world.

1. Compile a book of amazing achievements of students in your class.
    Almost anyone has

        been somewhere
        done something
        collects or owns something

    or

        met someone

    that no one else can claim.

2. Ask questions and record the answers.

3   Write and illustrate your book allowing one page for each amazing achievement. Some of your illustrations can be photographs if you have permission of those involved.

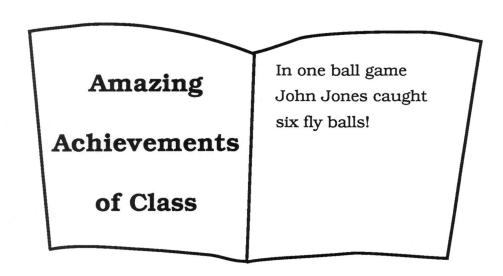

Amazing

Achievements

of Class

In one ball game
John Jones caught
six fly balls!

RECORD BOOKS!

WHAT'S THE BIGGEST?
By Barbara R. Fogel
Illustrated by Barbara Wolff
Random House, 1966

"WHAT'S THE BIGGEST?" explains
some surprising facts and theories
about bigness in man-made
things, in animals and men, on
earth and in the universe. The
author explores such questions as
these: What's the biggest living
reptile? What's the biggest
building? What's the biggest river?

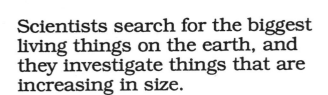

Scientists search for the biggest
living things on the earth, and
they investigate things that are
increasing in size.

Increase your vocabulary!

You are to conduct a search for
the biggest words. Use this model
to research and report your
findings.

Biggest Words From "A" To "Z"

To get you started:

A   antidisestablishmentarianism
B
C
D
E
F
G
H
I
J
K
L
M

N
O
P
Q
R
S
T
U
V
W
X
Y
Z

USING MEASUREMENT AS A REPORTING TOOL

Here is a great research model which gives interesting information in the form of measurement facts. Learn about the longest, tallest, oldest, youngest, and many more measurement facts! Use this model for reporting *your* research on an interesting topic. You may want to write THE LONGEST BOOK, or THE TALLEST BOOK or perhaps THE OLDEST BOOK! All of the information in your book will have to do with records on the measurement you have selected. For example: if you choose THE WIDEST BOOK you might include: 1. The widest river in your state. 2. The widest door in your school. 3. The widest country in the world. You can think of many more. Include an illustrated page for each fact you include.

HOW LONG?
To Go, To Grow, To Know
ROSS and PATRICIA OLNEY
Illustrated by R. W. ALLEY

Do you know how long it takes for your fingernails to grow a half an inch? How long does a giant sequoia tree live? Have you any idea how long it would take to get to the moon— if you had to walk? You'll find out in How Long? This easy-to-read book introduces young readers to the important relationship between time and change. Using fascinating comparisons, the simply written text explains that changes occur throughout nature at varying rates.

William Morrow, 1984

A Word Of Advice In Researching: Develop Very Specific Questions!

The more specific your question is, the easier it is to find the answer. For example: If your question is, "What is the longest river?" What do you really mean? The longest river in the world? The longest in your state? The longest in North America?

Examples Of Good Questions
What is the TALLEST building in Chicago?
Who is the HEAVIEST player playing in the National Football League today?
What is the WIDEST river in North America?

A BOOK OF WACKY FACTS

ENCYCLOPEDIA BROWN'S
BOOK OF WACKY SPIES
By DONALD J. SOBOL
Illustrated by TED ENIK
Morrow Junior Books 1984

Encyclopedia Brown is back, with a
zany new collection of tales from the
madcap world of espionage. Although
he's kept pretty busy through the
now-famous Brown Detective Agency,
Encyclopedia still finds time to gather
tales and trivia about wacky spies.
Followers of the dauntless young
sleuth can once again giggle and gasp
over the colorful exploits of spies both
inept and ingenious.

What a wonderful collection
of true but wacky facts about
spies throughout history!

Use this model as a way of
reporting research about the
town or city or state or
province in which you live!

Every community has its
funny or strange stories.
Many of the older residents of
the community could tell you
of strange and wacky things
that have happened over the
years.

Your local historical society
can provide letters, diaries,
and local histories as a
source for *your* book.

Sometimes, public libraries
have a local history section
where information is
available on both the usual
and the unusual happenings
of the area.

*You are sure to have a best
seller!*

What To Search For

Search for wacky facts about:
- Agriculture (crops, livestock etc.)
- Awards, medals
- Colleges, universities
- Corporations, businesses
- Disasters
- Discoveries, inventions
- Economics
- Education
- Elections
- Famous people

- Flags, names, mottos
- Landmarks
- Laws and documents
- Memorable dates
- Meteorological information (weather)
- Parks, amusement centers
- Population information (changes, etc.)
- Sports
- Surveys of resident preferences
- Any other topic you discover

ANIMAL ASSISTANT

Imagine that you own an unusual animal. How could you earn a living by utilizing that animal in a humane way?

1. What animal would you choose? _____

2. List ten traits of that animal:

   _____   _____
   _____   _____
   _____   _____
   _____   _____
   _____   _____

3. List ten things someone might hire the animal to do:

   _____   _____
   _____   _____
   _____   _____
   _____   _____
   _____   _____

4. Think of a business that would allow you to use the animal's traits to provide a needed service. Be as original as you can.

   _____

5. Write a job description telling what services you and the animal will provide, qualifications for both of you, and what you will charge.

   _____
   _____
   _____
   _____
   _____

A TIC-TAC-TOE REPORT

You can do a report on any topic using the format shown below. List nine questions about your topic. Provide a space for the user to answer the questions and to tell where the answer came from. Provide an answer key so that the user can check the answers he/she finds.

Tic-Tac-Toe With Dog Facts

Complete any three squares down, across, or diagonally. Use the books in the reference area to verify your answers. Identify your source in the square with the answer.

Name a breed suitable for training as a guide dog for the blind.	Tell one technique for training a dog to obey or do a trick.	List five characteristics of a responsible dog owner.
Name and describe one disease against which a dog needs protection.	Name one trait necessary for a guide dog.	What do you consider the most important criteria in choosing which breed of dog is the best pet?
Name one breed suitable for being a sled dog.	What traits and characteristics are vital for a sled dog?	Tell one instance when a dog is credited with saving a human's life.

Source:	Source:	Source:
Source:	Source:	Source:
Source:	Source:	Source:

THE LETTER REPORT

Select a problem that is currently in the news. Collect and read as many news articles about the problem as you can. After you have read the articles, form an opinion about the problem and what you believe would be steps in solving it. Write a letter to a government official (local, state or national) using the format below.

U. S. GOVERNMENT
(Your address)
(date)

The Honorable (_____)
name

the address

Dear Senator:

(The first paragraph will tell why you are writing and what your opinion is.)

(Other paragraphs should tell what the reasons are for your opinion.)

(In the closing paragraph you should summarize your ideas, restate your opinion, and thank the Senator for considering your opinion.)

Sincerely,

(Your name)

HOBBIES

PROJECT PLANNING

How could you turn one of your hobbies or special interests into a science fair project?

1. List your favorite hobbies or leisure activities:

   _____   _____
   _____   _____
   _____   _____

2. List pets, plants, animals, or insects found around your house:

   _____   _____
   _____   _____
   _____   _____

3. Choose one of these for a science fair project. What will your hypothesis be? What scientific concept will you try to demonstrate?

   _____
   _____
   _____

4. What materials will be needed?

   _____
   _____
   _____

5. What steps will you need to take?

   _____
   _____
   _____

6. What problems might you face?

   _____
   _____
   _____

BIOGRAPHY REPORTS
WITHOUT COPYING

by Virginia Mealy

Additional activities by Nancy Polette

illustrated by Paul Dillon

INTRODUCTION

This special section on Biography Reports Without Copying presents practical suggestions for using a particular literary form, the biography. These suggestions are designed to enrich the reading experiences of children in the elementary and middle school (or junior high school).

Biography is a vehicle for explorations which involve critical and creative thinking. These activity sheets are based on Bloom's levels of cognitive thinking, with emphasis on the three higher levels — analysis, synthesis, and evaluation.

Selecting good biographies is the teacher's and/or librarian's first task. In order to help in this process, several bibliographies have been developed under five very general subject headings: Men of Achievement, Women of Achievement, Sports Heroes and Heroines, People in Fine Arts and The Twentieth Century. Books selected for these bibliographies have been those recommended by authorities in the field of children's literature.

After a student has read a particular biography, the teacher and/or librarian may want the student to share his/her new knowledge. This wide variety of student activities permits flexibility, fluency, and originality. Hopefully, each page will present the student with new demands for thoughtful analysis and judgment in sharing his/her biographee's story.

Each page of this section has been developed in such a way that it will fit any biographee within a particular category. For example, the page entitled "Explanation, Please!" will work for any inventor, just as the page "Super Hero" will work for any one in the field of sports. Several of the pages have been developed on an even broader base regardless of the category. For example, the page "Party Time" can be used with <u>any</u> biographee.

The section on Biography Reports Without Copying presents activities which are limited only insofar as the teacher or librarian is limited in flexibility.

happiness is...

Happiness means different things to different people.

List five (5) things that make you happy.

1. _____

2. _____

3. _____

4. _____

5. _____

Suppose you had a chance to go back in time to another era and meet some well-known figures. Select three prominent figures from this time in history and write what you think each would tell you happiness means to them.

Historical Figure	Happiness is ...
1. _____ :	_____
	_____
2. _____ :	_____
	_____
3. _____ :	_____
	_____

Does the time in which people live change how they feel about what makes them happiest? _____ Explain:

_____

_____

_____

Plan the perfect party!

Pretend you are living during the time of
the biographee about whom you have
read. Plan all the details for this person's
birthday celebration.

Name of guest of honor _____

Who will you invite?   (These people must be living at the time of this
person's party.)

_____   _____

_____   _____

_____   _____

_____   _____

_____   _____

Where will the party be held?

_____

_____

What kind of decorations will you need? Describe them.

_____

_____

_____

_____

_____

On the back, design the invitation which you will send. Show the back as
well as the front of the invitation.

WRITE AN OBIT.

An <u>obituary</u> is found in a particular section of the newspaper. It is an official notice of a person's death, often accompanied by an account of his or her life and accomplishments.

Check the local newspaper for an example of an obituary.

Paste a sample here:

Many times a well-known person has a longer obituary which gives more information about his/her life and accomplishments.

Write the name of the person whose biography you have read.

_____

Write an obituary for this person. Be sure to tell some brief details of his/her life and at least two accomplishments.

_____

_____

_____

_____

_____

_____

_____

_____

ONE PERSON, ONE EPISODE

_____
Biographee's Name

- Select one event that happened during this person's lifetime.
- Explain in one sentence the reaction of this person to this event.
- Tell in one or two sentences what action the person took.
- Finally, briefly state the outcome of the action.

- Fill in the boxes with your information.

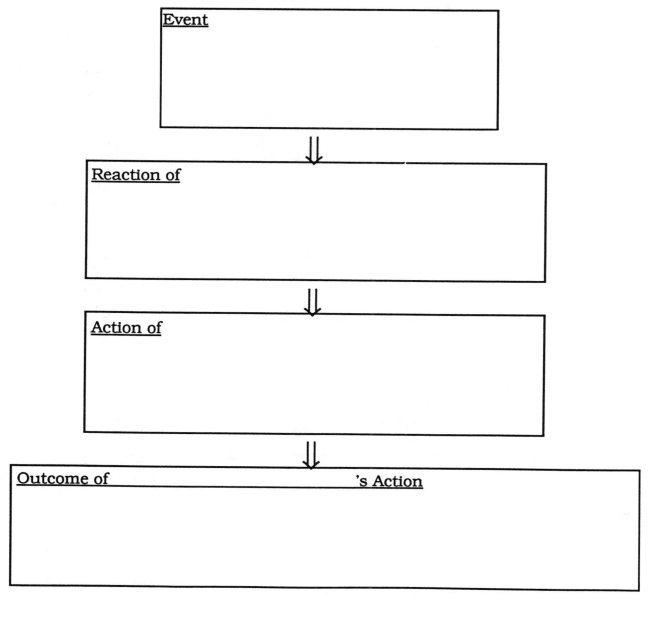

Event

⇓

Reaction of

⇓

Action of

⇓

Outcome of _____ 's Action

EXPLANATION, PLEASE!

Suppose you are the person you are today but because of a time warp you fall back in time to the days of the inventor whose biography you have read. You find yourself in this person's study.

You find that this inventor is very interested in something he/she has never seen before but with which you are very familiar. Explain something your inventor would have been interested in but which was not around in his/her lifetime. You may even want to draw a picture or a diagram of this "new" thing for your inventor.

Your inventor _____

Object in which he/she is interested _____

Your explanation:

_____

_____

_____

_____

_____

_____

_____

_____

Your picture or diagram:

A MONTH IN THE LIFE OF ...

Develop a calendar for one month in the life of the person whose biography you have read.

In this calendar include a variety of things that possibly happened as well as some things that did actually happen.

Biographee: _____

A MONTH IN THE LIFE OF

_____   _____

SUN	MON	TUE	WED	THU	FRI	SAT
		1	2	3	4	5
6	7	8	9	10	11	12
13	14	15	16	17	18	19
20	21	22	23	24	25	26
27	28	29	30			

CONSTRUCT A CROSSWORD

Use the grid below to create a crossword puzzle about a group of famous people in history who had something in common.

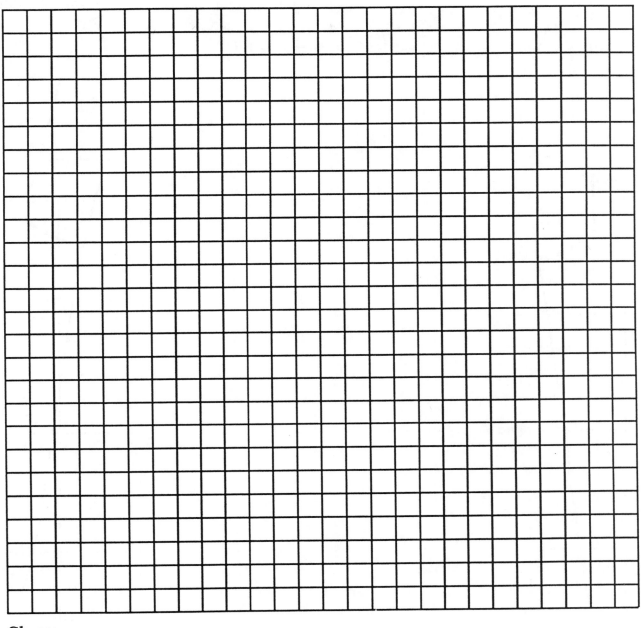

Clues:

Sloganed t-shirts are a 20th century craze. Often one learns a lot about an individual by reading the t-shirt he/she is wearing. Design a t-shirt that your biographee might have been proud to wear. Print a slogan that fits his/her personality and elaborate with a picture or other design.

Biographee _____

DESCRIBING BY COMPARING

Try to describe the person whose biography you have read through similes.

Name of Biographee _____

List adjectives which describe your biographee's personality, special qualities, and talents.

_____   _____   _____   _____

_____   _____   _____   _____

_____   _____   _____   _____

Now use these words to write five descriptive sentences about your biographee. Each sentence must contain a simile; a comparison using the words <u>like</u> or <u>as</u>.

EXAMPLE: Jim Thorpe ran as fast as the wind.

NOTE: Jim Thorpe and the wind are not alike except in one respect. They both possess a fleeting quality.

This device, the simile, helps the reader develop much better mental images about the biographee you are describing.

Write your similes below.

1. _____

_____

2. _____

_____

3. _____

_____

4. _____

_____

5. _____

_____

MY FAVORITE THINGS

Make a collage representing some of the favorite things of the person whose biography you have read. In this collage, you will add one extra feature. Beside or under each object, write a rhymed couplet about the drawing.

EXAMPLE: In a collage for Thomas Jefferson, there might be a drawing of a Spitzenburg apple, one of his favorites. Under it might appear two lines, such as:

Spitzenburg apples always pleased my taste;
In winter, my table they often graced.

_____ 'S FAVORITE THINGS

TIME CAPSULE

Name of Biographee _____

List things which are/were very important to your biographee.

_____   _____
_____   _____
_____   _____
_____   _____
_____   _____

Now select five of the things that this biographee might place in a time capsule for people to find one hundred years in the future. Attach a note to each one telling why this person thinks the item would have lasting significance.

EXAMPLE: John Chapman, also known as Johnny Appleseed left a small sack of apple seeds. His note says, "Plant these in good rich earth. They will bring forth a healthy, juicy fruit for future generations."

In the space below, list each of the five items selected and write a note to attach to each one.

CONTEMPORARIES

Weave a web of contemporaries. Show other famous people who lived at the same time as the person about whom you read.

EXAMPLE:

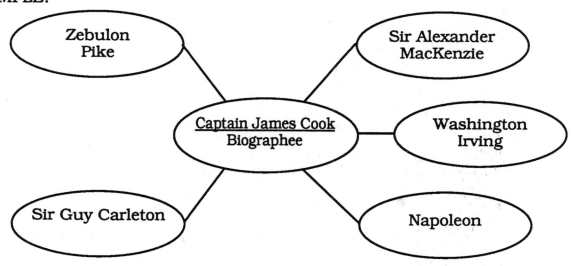

Weave your web. List your biographee in the center oval.

In the surrounding ovals, list four famous people who lived at the same time in history.

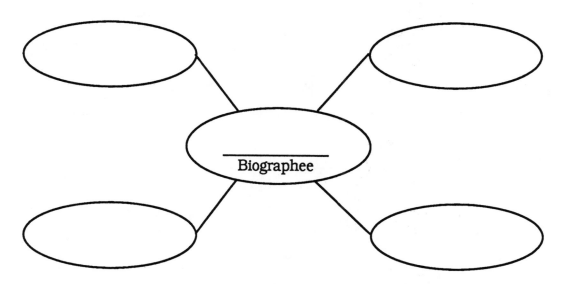

Now select one of the contemporaries of your biographee.

On the back write a conversation which might have taken place between your biographee and this contemporary.

LIFE PROBLEMS

Every man and woman faces problems in his/her lifetime. Some must make decisions which have far-reaching effects. For example, the famous scientist, Marie Curie, knew that working with radium was life-threatening. Yet the world would benefit if she continued her work.
What should she do? Consider the person about whom you read.

Biographee's name _____

What was one major decision this person had to make? Write the problem as a question.

_____

Now try to work through this problem. On the grid below, list ideas for three possible solutions and give two criteria for judging these ideas. Rate each.

What is the outcome of the grid? _____

_____

Is the solution you arrived at what this person did? _____ Explain.

_____

IDEAS Rate: 3 = yes 2 = maybe 1 = no	CRITERIA		TOTAL

Extra!
Extra!
Read ALL About It!

Clip words from your local newspaper to form a headline for a brief news story about a well-known figure in twentieth century history.

Make the story concise (your editor has limited you to no more than 100 words). Be sure to include the 5 W's ... who, what, when, where, why.

(Paste headline here.)

_____

_____

_____

_____

_____

_____

_____

_____

_____

_____

_____

_____

_____

_____

SUPER HEROES

In the world of sports there are many super heroes. Some achieve fame due to natural ability; others because of hard work. Think of a sports hero or heroine you have read about. Try telling about him or her in a song. Select a well-known melody such as "Row, Row, Row Your Boat" and tell about the sports person so that your words fit the tune.

Here is an example using "Row, Row, Row Your Boat" and Jessie Owens.

> Run, run, run, Jesse
> Run for the gold.
> Proudly, proudly, proudly, proudly,
> Your story will be told.

> Jump, jump, jump, Jesse
> Jump for the gold.
> Proudly, proudly, proudly, proudly,
> Your story will be told.

When you have completed your song, try singing it with some of your friends and present it to other groups.

Sport hero _____

Song _____

_____
_____
_____
_____
_____
_____
_____
_____

LEADERS

Canada and the United States have had many leaders. Write an acrostic poem about the President or Prime Minister whose biography you have read. Begin each line of the poem with the letters of the name itself.

Two examples are given below:

W as Prime Minister 21 years
L onger than any other

M ade efforts so that Canada
A chieved full status as a nation.
C anadian representative Imperial Conference 1926
K ept his interest in fair work laws
E ducation led to a series of
N ewspaper articles about conditions of
Z apped workers, low wages, long hours,
I ntended to better working man's lot
E conomic depression defeated him 1930

K ept trying, won in 35
I nsurance for unemployed achieved.
N oted for efficient
G overnment.

J ust at the time of America's need, there
E merged a multi-talented, red-haired Virginian,
F amed author of the Declaration of Independence,
F rankiln's sucessor as Minister to France.
E lected as Vice President and then President, he
R ecommended the purchase of the Louisianna Territory; then
S ent Lewis and Clark to explore the great Northwest.
O nly after 50 years of active public service did the
N ation's third President retire to Monticello.

Now try your own. Biographee _____

— _____
— _____
— _____
— _____
— _____
— _____
— _____
— _____
— _____
— _____
— _____

THE BIO-POEM

A bio-poem is one way to briefly tell about someone's life.

Here is an example.

Abraham

Tall, thin, lanky, bearded,

Son of Nancy and Tom, husband of Mary Todd, father of Robert, Edward, Willie and Tad.

Who cares deeply about all men,

Who feels sad much of the time, sometimes alone in the world,

Who needs to win the hearts of <u>all</u> his countrymen,

Who gives love to his family, advice to his generals, consolation to a sorrowing nation,

Who fears the dissolution of the American union,

Who would like to see every man respected for his God-given dignity,

Resident of 1600 Pennsylvania Avenue, Washington, D. C.

Now try one of your own. Select a person whose biography you have read and follow the pattern given below.

Line 1 - Name   _____

Line 2 - Four traits   _____

Line 3 - Related to   _____

Line 4 - Who cares deeply about   _____

Line 5 - Who feels   _____

Line 6 - Who needs   _____

Line 7 - Who gives   _____

Line 8 - Who fears   _____

Line 9 - Who would like to see   _____

Line 10 - Resident of   _____

MUSICAL CINQUAINS

A great deal can be said in a handful of words, but the words must be chosen with care and they must fit together in some form. This can be achieved by the cinquain, a short five-line poem of eleven words.

The form of the cinquain is:

Line 1	one word for the title
Line 2	two words describing the title
Line 3	three words that show action about the title
Line 4	four words (a phrase) that show feeling
Line 5	one word, a synonym for the title

Select someone from the world of music whose biography you have read. Write a cinquain about that personality. A sample is given here.

Bernstein
Energetic, Musical
Playing, Composing, Conducting
Spirit excited by music
Maestro

Write your cinquain on the lines below.

_____

_____

_____

_____

_____

What biography did you read? (Give author, title, and name of biographee.)

Biography: _____

Biographee: _____

WOMEN & DUTY

<u>Duty</u> has always been an important and not-to-be-ignored word in a woman's life. Write in the name of the woman whose biography you have read.

_____

List five (5) ways in which this woman chose to fulfill her duties in life as she saw them.

1. _____

_____

2. _____

_____

3. _____

_____

4. _____

_____

5. _____

_____

Select one of the ways you have written about and tell how this woman's life would have been different if she had not fulfilled this particular duty.

_____

_____

_____

_____

REBEL ROUSERS

Many famous people have been put in jail because of their strong beliefs which were contrary to those of the time in which they lived. Among these famous names are:

NELLIE BLY

DANIEL DE FOE

O. HENRY

MARY HARRIS JONES

MARCO POLO

SIR WALTER RALEIGH

HENRY DAVID THOREAU

The person you have selected (either from this list or another person not on the list) has become known today as "A Rebel" because of something that happened in his or her lifetime.

Write a story about his or her life in which you show how this person could be called "A Rebel."

BIOGRAPHEE _____

5 FT

4 FT

POLICE DEPT.
477601

_____
_____
_____
_____
_____
_____
_____
_____
_____
_____

THE MYSTERY PERSON BIOGRAPHY REPORT #1

Here is a fun way to report on the life of a famous person!

1. Read a biography.

2. List eighteen things you discovered about the person. Number from one to eighteen.

3. In listing these "clues" include one or two very easy ones. The others give interesting information about the person.

4. PLAY THE MYSTERY PERSON GAME!

Directions: Each contestant selects three numbers (one at a time). The reader reads the clue for each number. After each clue, the contestant can make one guess as to who the mystery person is. If the contestant does not guess correctly after three clues, another contestant selects three clues and has three guesses. The game continues until six contestants have had a try at selecting clues and guessing or until the mystery person is discovered.

CLUE#

1. My mother was a famous American beauty.
2. My grandfather was a Duke.
3. I won many medals for valor.
4. I did poorly in school.
5. At one time in my life I was a newspaper correspondent.
6. I was captured by the Boers in South Africa but managed to escape.
7. I served in the British Parliament.
8. I was a writer and lecturer.
9. My wife's name was Clementine.
10. I was First Lord of the Admirality in World War One.
11. I learned to fly within ten years of the invention of the airplane.
12. I was Lieutenant Colonel in World War One.
13. I founded the Royal Naval Air Service.
14. I helped establish the State of Iraq in 1921.
15. I was a painter.
16. In 1931 I toured and lectured in the United States.
17. In 1940 I succeeded Neville Chamberlain as Prime Minister of Great Britain.
18. I met with FDR nine times and sent him 1700 messages.

(Answer is on page 124)

MYSTERY PERSON BIOGRAPHY REPORT #2

Directions: Each contestant selects three numbers (one at a time). The reader reads the clue for each number. After each clue, the contestant can make one guess as to who the mystery person is. If the contestant does not guess correctly after three clues, another contestant selects three clues and has three guesses. The game continues until six contestants have had a try at selecting clues and guessing or until the mystery person is discovered.

CLUE#

1. My mother was the first woman to reach the top of Pike's Peak.
2. The caption under my high school graduation picture read: "The girl in brown who walks alone."
3. A mystery surrounds my death.
4. I believe that people should dare to live and that comfort and security are poor goals in life.
5. I was born in Atchinson, Kansas.
6. I never liked my first name and preferred to be called by my initials.
7. During World War One I served as a nurse's aide in a Toronto hospital for veterans.
8. As a child I enjoyed building things like chicken traps and roller coasters.
9. I wanted to prove that given a choice, women could achieve what men had achieved.
10. I married George Putnam, a well-known publisher.
11. I was the first woman to cross the Atlantic Ocean by air.
12. As a child I was called a tomboy and deserved the name.
13. I was the first woman to receive the Distinguished Flying Cross.
14. I attended Columbia University but did not graduate from college.
15. My father was an alcoholic and I spent much of my childhood with my grandparents.
16. These words of mine are often quoted: "Hooray for the last adventure!"
17. To keep from getting lost, I would often pin maps on my collar.
18. I once slept in a leather jacket for five nights to get the newness out of it.

(Answer on page 124)

THE TELEVISION SHOW BIOGRAPHY REPORT

Report on the life of a famous person using the TO TEST THE TRUTH television script model that follows. Note that in the model, three people pretend to be the real famous person. Only one of the famous persons gives absolutely correct answers. The other two do not always tell the truth. At the end of the script the audience (your classmates) vote on which is the real famous person.

TO TEST THE TRUTH

Characters:
Larry or Loretta Bore, host
Three Panelists
Three Mary Kingsleys
Jury (Audience)

BORE:
Welcome everyone! Let me explain what is going to happen on our show today. We have three panelists who will try to guess which of our three guests is telling the truth about herself. Only one is a famous writer/explorer. The others are imposters. It is up to the audience to determine the real writer/explorer. Now let's meet our guests.

BORE:
Number One. What is your name?

NUMBER ONE:
My name is Mary Kingsley.

BORE:
Number Two. What is your name?

NUMBER ONE:
My name is Mary Kingsley.

BORE:
Number Three. What is your name?

NUMBER ONE:
My name is Mary Kingsley.

BORE: Let's listen to Mary Kingsley's story.

NUMBER ONE:
I, Mary Kingsley, was born October 17, 1862 in London, England. My mother was a former domestic servant and barely literate.

NUMBER TWO:
My father was a physician, a scientist and a writer and instilled early in me a passion for learning.

NUMBER THREE:
My mother was a chronic invalid so rather than getting an education, I spent much of my early life taking care of her.

BORE:
Now it's up to our panelists to "Test the Truth." Let's begin with Panelist Number One.

PANELIST NUMBER ONE:
Kingsley Number One: If you received no education as a child, how did you acquire the skills you needed to become a famous writer?

NUMBER ONE:
While my mother was not concerned with education, my father was very concerned. He taught both my brother and me at home. We studied physics, chemistry, Latin, zoology and anthropology among other subjects.

PANELIST NUMBER ONE:
Kingsley Number Two: I understand that you idolized your father. Would you tell us about him?

NUMBER TWO:
He was a great man. His passion was to travel to far away places and he often took me with him. Upon our return, it was my job to put his notes in order for the great book on his travels he was going to write.

PANELIST NUMBER ONE:
Kingsley Number Three: Did you consider yourself to be a fairly bright young woman?

NUMBER THREE:
Quite the opposite. I always considered myself dumb as well as a misfit. I spoke Cockney English and people often laughed at me for dropping my "h's".

BORE:
That's it for Panelist Number One. Now let's hear from Panelist Number Two.

PANELIST NUMBER TWO:
Kingsley Number One: How did you manage to become a famous African explorer?

NUMBER ONE:
When I was 30 my parents died within six weeks of each other. I had always wanted to travel, so with a grant from the London Society I set out to explore and write about parts of Africa.

PANELIST NUMBER TWO:
Kingsley Number Two: Tell us about some of your explorations.

NUMBER TWO:
Well, I shocked England, I'll tell you by wearing men's clothes but how else can one manage narrow jungle trails, chop one's way through a rain forest, sleep on the floor of a tribal hut, paddle a canoe through rapids and pilot a ship up West African creeks?

PANELIST NUMBER TWO:
Kingsley Number Three: Can you tell us of at least one memorable experience of your travels?

NUMBER THREE:
There was the day I fell into a game pit lined at the bottom with ivory spikes. The only thing that allowed me to emerge alive was the thick folds of my gown over ample petticoats that caught the spikes instead of my skin!

BORE:
Now it's time to hear from Panelist Number Three.

PANELIST NUMBER THREE:
Kingsley Number One: What were the main purposes of your travels?

NUMBER ONE:
To study fish and fetish...that is the religion of the people...and to help African women to achieve equality with their men.

PANELIST NUMBER THREE:
Kingsley Number Two: Who helped you the most in your travels?

NUMBER TWO:
The traders, of course. The Africans were their customers and they knew how important it was to understand their customer's needs, thoughts and feelings. Missionaries were helpful as well for they had a deep understanding of the people.

PANELIST NUMBER THREE:
Kingsley Number Three: It was said

that you set English tongues to wagging when you returned from Africa to lecture. Why was this?

NUMBER THREE:
The English Government said the African native should have one wife and no whiskey. I was outraged and said so. There is no place in Africa for an unmarried woman and without polygamy, thousands of women would starve to death. Then too, I'd like to see some of those fancy London officials spend weeks in the fever-filled heat of the tropics without an occasional swig of whiskey.

BORE:
Our time is up for questions and the panelists and jury will have to vote. Panelist Number One, cast your vote.

PANELIST NUMBER ONE:
(Casts vote for his/her choice)

BORE:
Panelist Number Two, cast your vote.

PANELIST NUMBER TWO:
(Casts vote for his/her choice)

BORE:
Panelist Number Three, cast your vote.

PANELIST NUMBER THREE:
(Casts vote for his/her choice)

BORE:
Now it is time for the jury (audience) to vote by a show of hands.
It is Number One?
Is it Number Two?
Is it Number Three?

BORE:
Will the real Mary Henrietta Kingsley world-famous African explorer, writer and lecturer please step forward.

NOTE: In order to discover which Mary Kingsley is telling the truth you will need to read about her life. Which one is the real Mary Kingsley??????

To discover who is telling the truth, read: African Traveler by Ronald Syme.

(See answer key for this script on page 124)

Selected Bibliography: Outstanding Biographies

MEN OF ACHIEVEMENT

Aliki (Brandenberg). <u>A Weed Is A Flower, The Life Of George Washington Carver</u>. Prentice-Hall, 1965.

d'Aulaire, Ingri and Edgar Parin d'Aulaire. <u>Christopher Columbus</u>. Doubleday, 1955.

Brenner, Barbara. <u>On The Frontier With Mr. Audubon</u>. Coward McCann, 1977.

Clayton, Ed. <u>Martin Luther King: The Peaceful Warrior</u>, 3rd ed. Prentice-Hall, 1968.

DeTrevino, Elizabeth Borton. <u>I, Juan de Pareja</u>. Farrar, Straus, 1965.

Faber, Doris. <u>I Will Be Heard, The Life of William Lloyd Garrison.</u> Lothrop, 1970.

Fecher, Constance. <u>The Last Elizabethan, A Portrait of Sir Walter Raleigh</u>. Farrar, Straus, 1972.

Franchere, Ruth. <u>Cesar Chavez</u>. Crowell, 1970.

Fritz, Jean. <u>And Then What Happened, Paul Revere?</u> Coward McCann, 1973.

Fritz, Jean. <u>Can't You Make Them Behave, King George?</u> Coward McCann, 1976.

Fritz, Jean. <u>Traitor: The Case of Benedict Arnold</u>. Putnam, 1981.

Fritz, Jean. <u>What's The Big Idea, Ben Franklin?</u> Coward McCann, 1976.

Fritz, Jean. <u>Where Do You Think You're Going, Christopher Columbus?</u> Putnam, 1980.

Fritz, Jean. <u>Why Don't You Get A Horse, Sam Adams?</u> Coward McCann, 1974.

Fritz, Jean. <u>Will You Sign Here, John Hancock?</u> Coward McCann, 1976.

Goodsell, Jane. <u>The Mayo Brothers</u>. Crowell, 1972.

Hardwick, Richard. <u>Charles Richard Drew, Pioneer In Blood Research.</u> Scribner, 1967.

Judson, Clara Ingram. <u>Thomas Jefferson, Champion Of The People.</u> Follett, 1952.

Lawson, Robert. <u>Ben And Me.</u> Little-Brown, 1951 (1939).

Lawson, Robert. <u>Mr. Revere And I.</u> Little-Brown, 1953.

Levine, I. E. <u>Young Man In The White House, John Fitzgerald Kennedy.</u> Washington Square Press, 1969 (1964).

Neimark, Anne E. <u>Touch Of Light, The Story Of Louis Braille.</u> Harcourt Brace Jovanovich, 1970.

Provensen, Alice, and Martin Provensen. <u>The Glorious Flight: Across The Channel With Louis Bleriot.</u> Viking, 1983.

Rosen, Sidney. <u>Wizard Of The Dome: R. Buckminster Fuller, Designer Of The Future.</u> Little-Brown, 1969.

Syme, Ronald. <u>Cartier Of The St. Lawrence.</u> Morrow, 1958.

Syme, Ronald. <u>Juarez, The Founder Of Modern Mexico.</u> Morrow, 1972.

Syme, Ronald. <u>Vasco da Gama, Sailor Toward The Sunrise.</u> Morrow, 1959.

Syme, Ronald. <u>Verrazano, Explorer Of The Atlantic Coast.</u> Morrow, 1973.

Yates, Elizabeth. <u>Amos Fortune, Free Man.</u> Dutton, 1950.

Selected Bibliography: Outstanding Biographies

SPORTS HEROES AND HEROINES

Brondfield, Jerry. Hank Aaron ... 714 And Beyond. Scholastic, 1974.

Buchard, S. H. Wayne Gretzky. Harcourt, 1982.

Fall, Thomas. Jim Thorpe. Crowell, 1970.

Hano, Arnold. Kareem! Basketball Great. Putnam, 1975.

Kaufman, Mervyn. Jesse Owens. Crowell, 1973.

Olsen, James T. Billie Jean King, The Lady Of The Court. Creative Education (Children's Press), 1974.

Sullivan, George. Willie Mays. Putnam, 1973.

United Press International. Clemente. Grosset & Dunlap, 1973.

WOMEN OF ACHIEVEMENT

Baker, Rachel. America's First Trained Nurse: Linda Richards. Washington Square Press, 1970 (1959).

Bigland, Eileen. Madame Curie. Criterion Books, 1957.

Brown, Marion, and Ruth Crone. The Silent Storm. Abingdon Press, 1963.

Brownmiller, Susan. Shirley Chisholm, A Biography. Doubleday, 1970.

Chaffin, Lillie, and Miriam Butwin. America's First Ladies 1789 to 1965. Lerner, 1969.

Davidson, Mickie. Helen Keller's Teacher. Four Winds, 1965.

Dobrin, Arnold. A Life For Israel, The Story Of Golda Meir. Dial, 1974.

Epstein, Sam, and Beryl Epstein. She Never Looked Back: Margaret Mead In Samoa. Coward McCann, 1980.

Faber, Doris. Eleanor Roosevelt, First Lady Of The World. Viking Kestrel, 1985.

Faber, Doris. Love And Rivalry: Three Exceptional Pairs Of Sisters. Viking, 1983.

Felton, Harold W. Mumbet, The Story Of Elizabeth Freeman. Dodd Mead, 1970.

Fox, Mary Virginia. Lady For The Defense, A Biography Of Belva Lockwood. Harcourt Brace Jovanovich, 1975.

Graham, Shirley. The Story Of Phillis Wheatley, Poetess Of The American Revolution. Washington Square Press, 1969.

Greenfield, Eloise. Mary McLeod Bethune. Crowell, 1977.

Hicks, Nancy. The Honorable Shirley Chisholm, Congresswoman From Brooklyn. Lion, 1971.

Hunter, Edith F. Child Of The Silent Night. Houghton Mifflin, 1963.

Keller, Mollie. Marie Curie. Franklin Watts, 1982.

Latham, Jean Lee. Rachel Carson: Who Loved The Sea. Garrard, 1973.

Lauber, Patricia. Lost Star: Story Of Amelia Earhart. Scholastic Books, 1988.

Lawrence, Jacob. Harriet And The Promised Land. Windmill, 1968.

Longsworth, Polly. I, Charlotte Forten, Black And Free. Crowell, 1977.

McGovern, Ann. The Secret Soldier: The Story Of Deborah Sampson. FourWinds, 1975.

Selected Bibliography: Outstanding Biographies

WOMEN OF ACHIEVEMENT (continued)

Meltzer, Milton. <u>Dorothea Lange: Life Through The Camera.</u> Viking, 1985.

Peare, Catherine Owens. <u>The Helen Keller Story.</u> Crowell, 1959.

Selden, Bernice. <u>The Mill Girls.</u> Atheneum, 1983.

Sterling, Dorothy. <u>Freedom Train, The Story Of Harriet Tubman.</u> Doubleday, 1954.

Stevens, Bryna. <u>Deborah Sampson Goes To War.</u> Carolrhoda Books, 1984.

Syme, Ronald. <u>African Traveler, The Story Of Mary Kingsley.</u> Morrow, 1962.

Syme, Ronald. <u>Nigerian Pioneer. The Story Of Mary Slessor.</u> Morrow, 1964.

THE FINE ARTS

Aldis, Dorothy. <u>Nothing Is Impossible, The Story Of Beatrix Potter.</u> Atheneum, 1969.

Barth, Edna. <u>I'm Nobody! Who Are You? The Story Of Emily Dickinson.</u> Seabury, 1971.

Blair, Gwenda. <u>Laura Ingalls Wilder.</u> Putnam, 1981.

Blegvad, Erik. <u>Self-Portrait: Erik Blegvad.</u> Addison-Wesley, 1979.

Cone, Molly. <u>Leonard Bernstein.</u> Crowell, 1970.

DeLeeuw, Adele. <u>Maria Tallchief, American Ballerina.</u> Garrard, 1971.

Duncan, Lois. <u>Chapters: My Growth As A Writer.</u> Little-Brown, 1982.

Fisher, Aileen, and Olive Rabe. <u>We Alcotts.</u> Atheneum, 1968.

Fisher, Aileen, and Olive Rabe. <u>We Dickinsons.</u> Atheneum, 1965.

Fritz, Jean. <u>Homesick: My Own Story.</u> Putnam, 1982.

Haverstock, Mary Sayre. <u>Indian Gallery. The Story Of George Catlin.</u> Four Winds, 1973.

Jackson, Jesse. <u>Make A Joyful Noise Unto The Lord! The Life Of Mahalia Jackson, Queen Of Gospel Singers.</u> Crowell, 1974.

Jones, Hettie. <u>Big Star Fallin' Mama: Five Women In Black Music.</u> Viking, 1974.

Kelen, Emery. <u>Mr. Nonsense. A Life Of Edward Lear.</u> Norton, 1973.

Lasker, David. <u>The Boy Who Loved Music.</u> Viking, 1979.

Lenski, Lois. <u>Journey Into Childhood. The Autobiography Of Lois Lenski.</u> Lippincott, 1972.

McNeer, May. <u>America's Mark Twain.</u> Houghton Mifflin, 1962.

Mathis, Sharon Bell. <u>Ray Charles.</u> Crowell, 1973.

Meltzer, Milton. <u>Langston Hughes. A Biography.</u> Crowell, 1968.

Raboff, Ernest. <u>Marc Chagall.</u> Doubleday, 1968.

Raboff, Ernest. <u>Pablo Picasso.</u> Doubleday, 1968.

Raboff, Ernest. <u>Paul Klee.</u> Doubleday, 1968.

Rockwell, Anne. <u>The Boy Who Drew Sheep.</u> Atheneum, 1973.

Rockwell, Anne. <u>Paintbrush & Peacepipe: The Story Of George Catlin.</u> Atheneum, 1971.

Tobias, Tobi. <u>Marian Anderson.</u> Crowell, 1972.

Wojciechowska, Maia. <u>Till The Break Of Day. Memories 1939-1942.</u> Harcourt Brace Jovanovich, 1972.

Zemach, Margot. <u>Self-Portrait: Margot Zemach.</u> Addison-Wesley, 1978.

Selected Bibliography: Outstanding Biographies

THE TWENTIETH CENTURY WORLD

Adoff, Arnold. Malcom X. Crowell, 1970.

Behrens, June. Sally Ride, Astronaut: An American First. Children's Press, 1984.

Clayton, Ed. Martin Luther King: The Peaceful Warrior. 3rd ed. Prentice-Hall, 1968.

Commager, Henry Steele, ed. Franklin D. Roosevelt And The New Deal. Children's Press, 1987.

Devaney, John. Hitler, Mad Dictator Of World War II. Putnam, 1978.

Dobrin, Arnold. A Life For Israel, The Story Of Golda Meir. Dial, 1974.

Epstein, Sam, and Beryl Epstein. Enrico Fermi: Father Of Atomic Power. Garrard, 1970.

Epstein, Sam, and Beryl Epstein. Winston Churchill: Lion Of Britain. Garrard, 1971.

Faber, Doris. Eleanor Roosevelt, First Lady Of The World. Viking Kestrel, 1985.

Franchere, Ruth. Cesar Chavez. Crowell, 1970.

Greenfield, Eloise. Mary McLeod Bethune. Crowell, 1977.

Greenfield, Eloise. Rosa Parks. Crowell, 1973.

Haskins, Jim and Kathleen Benson. Space Challenger: The Story Of Guion Bluford. Carolrhoda Books, 1984.

Hoyt, Mary Finch. American Woman Of The Space Age. Atheneum, 1966.

Montgomery, Elizabeth. Albert Schweitzer: Great Humanitarian. Garrard, 1971.

Richards, Kenneth G. Charles Lindbergh. Children's Press, 1968.

Sullivan, George. Sadat: The Man Who Changed Mid-East History. Walker, 1981.

Wojciechowska, Maia. Till The Break Of Day, Memories: 1939-1942. Harcourt, 1972.

ANSWERS

Page 117 — Winston Churchill

Page 118 — Amelia Earhart

Page 119-120 — The real Mary Kingsley is Number Three:
    Mary was not taught by her father.
    She never travelled with him.
    She never received a travel grant.
    She never wore men's clothes.
    She was not concerned with equality for African women.
    She felt missionaries did more harm than good.